TYBEE ISLAND

HEROES AND HOOLIGANS

The Making of an Island Paradise, Vol. 1

J.R. Roseberry

Cover Art: front cover photo is of Albert Seidl painting the Tybee Island Lighthouse by J.R.Roseberry; back cover photo is Tybee Island Beach by Lauren Clackum.

Paperback ISBN: 978-1-959563-03-7
Hardback ISBN: 978-1-959563-05-1
eBook ISBN: 978-1-959563-04-4

Published by:
Maudlin Pond Press
P.O. Box 53
Tybee Island, GA 31328

www.maudlinpond.com

Dedicated to my sisters, Jackie Eggerton, left, and Mary Lib Saleh, standing with me beside the park in Highlands, NC, which is named for our mother, Martha P. Neese, to whom this book is also dedicated, along with the myriad other women (you know who you are) who have helped me navigate this wayward life.

Preface

I was in my early 20s when Tybee seduced me.

Situated just down the road from Savannah, more than a few things about the island turned my head.

Her beauty was ubiquitous, from her willowy, windswept dunes to her miles of pristine beach bordering, depending on her mood, either crashing or calmly serene surf, it was a photographer's paradise.

It was paradise in other ways as well for an energetic young reporter for the Savannah Morning News.

Populated by eccentric, hard-drinking party-lovers, its raucous bars made Tybee the polar opposite of what was then Savannah's sleepy ambience.

Preachers and politicians, scions of society and scallywags, lawyers, gamblers, fishermen, musicians, and artists rubbed shoulders on its beaches and in its bistros.

I fell in love with the island, deeply and permanently.

The job at the Savannah newspaper was my first since leaving Tokyo, where from 1957 to 1960 I had pursued post graduate studies in philosophy while working for Pacific Stars & Stripes, the Associated Press and the Okinawa Morning Star.

My shift at the newspaper, covering city hall before being named editor of Savannah Magazine, was from 3 p.m. to 11 p.m. or so, depending on the events of the day.

When my workday ended, there was little happening in Savannah, where only one bar, the Port Royal, was then operating on River Street.

In contrast, Tybee's bars were alive and filled with music-loving, beer-guzzling locals who were quick to befriend anyone on an adjacent bar stool at face value, rarely asking where they were from or what they did for a living.

After hoisting a few, the natives often regaled you with tales of Tybee's past, some of which had an ominous edge.

Semi-inebriated islanders said there had been no rapes or murders on Tybee for years because most miscreants knew how locals dealt with such felonies.

Their stories described how they'd drag malevolent offenders aboard a shrimp boat and drop them off the stern when the shrimpers lowered their nets while heading out to sea.

For lesser offenses like robberies or break-ins, culprits might be hauled over to Little Tybee, buried up to their chests in the sand, have honey poured on their heads, and be left to try to extricate themselves before ants and gulls had a picnic.

I never knew whether the tales were true or simply cautionary warnings, but, like others who heard them, I was not inclined to find out.

With no mandated closing time, Tybee's beach-side bacchanal often lasted till dawn, providing stress relief and a plethora of new pleasures enlivening my existence and expanding my horizons.

More often than many mature folks might find reasonable, I found myself driving back to Savannah with eyes watering from the burning sunrise reflected in the rear-view mirror.

Those were the "good old days" I found on Tybee 62 years ago, before heading north to continue my newspaper career with the Norfolk Virginian-Pilot from 1962 to 1967 and the Washington Post from 1967 to 1992.

Based on that early exposure to Tybee, when it came time to retire from the Post, I headed back to the island, looking for the good vibes I remembered to help me decide what I wanted to do with the rest of my life and where I wanted to do it.

My plan was to hunker down near the beach for a month to get my head around such stuff. That was 30 years ago, and I never left.

Once I realized I was here to stay, I expanded my interests well beyond those initial bar-hopping days.

I joined the "Y" and helped start a senior's club there; joined four friends in initiating the annual New Year's Day Polar Bear Plunge which now draws thousands; promoted the first official and now annual New Year's Eve celebration on the South End; helped salvage the old Post Theater when it was about to be demolished; and helped create a DeSoto Beach Hotel exhibit in the Lighthouse Museum to preserve memories of the island's storied old Mediterranean-style hotel.

Along the way I met dozens of islanders who had lived and were still living extraordinary lives and became convinced that their stories should be shared before they were lost forever.

Early (circa 1997) fan Mary Slater enjoys Closeup column with morning smoke and coffee.

Bitten once again by the writing bug, I started a weekly column in what was then the Savannah newspaper's "Closeup" section called "J.R.'s Island View." The column introduced readers to often little-known but fascinating folks who lived on or near Tybee Island.

The columns not only described their impressive accomplishments but told of their escapades and foibles. Based on the positive feedback from readers, the column succeeded in providing its audience with a bit of informative and refreshing reading over morning coffee.

Since becoming somewhat more reflective as I've grown considerably longer in the tooth, it occurred to me that those stories, collectively, captured a snapshot of what Tybee was like a quarter century ago.

Many long-time Tybee residents now believe those were the "real" good old days.

This book is a compilation of some those old columns and photos.

They've been assembled in the hope that they may help those who were here at the time savor some pleasant memories and may provide newcomers with a slice of easy-to-swallow island history.

For recent island arrivals, I suspect today will become their own good old days when they think about them 25 years from now, years that will pass far faster than most can imagine.

With luck, the current crop of writers will help them enjoy these treasured memories one day, just as I'm hoping to do with this book.

POSTSCRIPT: You will see postscripts after most

chapters to let you know what has happened to the folks I've written about since I first put their stories to paper.

Some have passed away or moved away, and some have vanished without a trace (that is, without giving me a chance to put them into my witness protection).

If you have information that I do not, please send it my way to P.O. Box 1503, Tybee Island, GA 31328 or jayrose@juno.com.

Table of Contents

Nickie Alexander - The Last of the Island Kingpins

Most Folks Knew Not to Mess with This Old Boy

Most newcomers to Tybee Island know him simply as the familiar but somewhat shadowy figure who until recently spent most days seated at a desk behind the large window of his bail bond office on Butler Avenue, near its intersection with Tybrisa Street.

Several huge, clear glass jugs weighing an estimated 200 pounds each and containing thousands of pennies stood like sentinels in the window somehow signaling this was the place to come if you weren't on the best of terms with regular financial institutions; were in trouble with the law or were just down on your luck.

He never worried that any of the down and out, often inebriated passersby would smash a window to grab one of the jars or try to rob him of the considerable cash many knew he kept in the office. No one would dare!

Few knew exactly why, but it was common knowledge that you just didn't mess around with Nicholas "Nickie" Alexander.

What relatively recent arrivals don't know is that Nickie is the last of the bistro kingpins who changed the face of the island during its wide-open, rough-and-tumble heyday following World War II.

Originally from Youngstown, Ohio, Nickie first set foot on the island as a young soldier in 1944 when he came to visit his older brother, Benny, who was operating the Rip Tide bar near the beach on the south end of the island.

Benny was also the front man for several famous orchestras at the time, including the Glen Gray Casa Loma Band, and was the first person to book a major band on the island's old Pavilion.

"When I got to Savannah, it cost me seven bucks to take a cab to the island," Nickie recalls. "That was big money at the time."

Back then, there was no wide expanse of sand on the south-end beach beside Strand Avenue, which was known as "The Front," a name still used by the handful of old timers who are still around.

There was no visible sand at all in that area at high tide, according to Nickie, who says there was a boardwalk bordering a high sea wall from which fishermen would cast their lines into the waves that lapped it when the tide was in.

Despite the absence of the wide beach that now draws thousands to Tybee from all over the country, there were actually more attractions offered to keep visitors entertained at that time.

The old Pavilion and property adjoining it sported a wide variety of venues, and Nickie recalls a constant parade of big bands performing on the Pavilion each evening throughout the summer.

He says droves of dancers whirled the night away to the music of Benny Goodman, the Dorsey brothers, and other famous groups whose music filled the warm summer air, caressing both the dancers and the hundreds of strollers along the nearby boardwalk.

On sunny days, folks flocked to the beach from Savannah in their jalopies or aboard Trailways buses, which arrived every hour on the half hour, stopping at the station near Butler Avenue and 16th Street.

Huge jars filled with pennies line Nickie's office window.

"Most people rode the bus back then," says Nickie. "There weren't that many cars. The road out was just a narrow two lanes. In September you could drive all the way to town and never pass another car."

Beach goers who were not relaxing on the sand at low tide could usually be found playing "half rubber," a popular beach game in which a broom stick was used as a bat to hit an erratically sailing half of a solid rubber ball. The sea wall served as a natural backstop for the game.

A bath house and a carnival featuring a Ferris wheel and carousel with solid wood horses was situated on the land end of the Pavilion, and there was a bowling alley on top of the bath house.

Visitors left their street clothes in the bath house lockers and rented one-piece, black wool bathing suits. The swimsuits covered both men and women from shoulders to thighs.

"In those days you could give a guy at the parking lot at the foot of 16th Street a quarter and you could park there all day," recalls Nickie.

He says one surprisingly modern diversion, helicopter tours, was also available in the 1950s. The helicopters took off and landed in an empty field beside the boardwalk at the beach end of 15th Street. "You'd pay $7.50, and it would take you all around the island."

"Nickie's," a little beer-and-pizza joint near the spot where the flights took place, was the first business he started on Tybee.

Nearby was the Ocean Plaza, which was then a ten-room motel not far from the classic old Tybee Hotel, a multi-storied structure covering most of the land between 14th and 15th Streets.

"That was a fine old hotel, and it was strong, built of solid stone," he says. "That's where people would go when there was a hurricane."

The old wooden Pavilion was clearly not the place to be in a big blow. It took a pounding in the hurricane of 1947, back before they started naming such storms.

"It was battered by that storm and huge pilings from the pier washed up onto 16th Street (now Tybrisa Street) where water was hip deep," according to Nickie.

In the 1960s, after the last of the big bands – "It was Ted Weems," he recalls - played there, the Pavilion fell into disrepair, and the old dance floor was converted into a skating rink for a while.

It met its final demise in 1968 in the biggest case of arson in the island's history - a case which remains officially unsolved to this day, although there are some old-timers apparently know better.

Fire departments from Garden City, Thunderbolt, and

Savannah responded to the fire which destroyed the Pavilion, pier, and a number of businesses along The Front, including the Rip Tide bar, the bowling alley, the bath house, and the top floor of what was then a two-story Christy's restaurant.

"An 18-year-old boy who was working on the roof got mad because he didn't get paid and set the place on fire," according to Nickie. "I don't remember who it was. I never did try to find out."

It appears that island authorities didn't try very hard either. They never charged anyone with the crime although there are those who say they know who the arsonist was and that the culprit still lives on the island.

At the height of the fire Nickie says he helped wet down merchandise in the T.S. Chu Department Store with a fire hose to save it from the blaze.

He was an admirer of the famous store's founder, T.S. Chu, who started what has become one of the largest business conglomerates on the island, with a hot dog stand beside the beach in the 1930s.

"He was a fine man," says Nickie. "He helped and was really good to a lot of people on the island."

Attractions for islanders and tourists were not all relegated to the south end in those days.

A par-three golf course and a raised restaurant were

situated just outside the pillars marking the entrance to Ft. Screven on the north end, and just up the street from those was the Beach Theater.

The theater was considered one of the best and most modern movie houses in the country at the time and is believed to be the first in the state to offer movies with sound, which were then called "talkies."

The building is now the subject of a concerted restoration effort after having been acquired by the Tybee Historical Society several years ago when the previous owner threatened to demolish it and build condos on the site.

Day-trippers usually left the beach early in those days while making sure they ate early as well, according to Nickie, who says, "if you didn't eat by 7 o'clock, you didn't eat nowhere. There wasn't a restaurant open after that time, and there was only one gas station which closed at 6 o'clock."

In addition to family entertainment there was money to be made in restaurant, bar, and gambling venues, and Nickie, who admits he had little interest in traditional family recreational activities, was determined to get his share of it.

"I kept my head pretty much to business all the time," he says, noting that he worked as a bartender at most of Tybee's bars as well as at the Club Royale, a famous Savannah nightclub located where a drug store is now situated at the corner of Victory Drive and Skidaway Road.

His brother Benny, along with Al Remler and former Tybee Mayor Jimmy Brown, owned the nightclub, where nationally-known entertainers frequently performed.

"I still remember when Harry James and his orchestra played there," says Nickie. "He was the most famous and got the most money, but there was also Tommy and Jimmy Dorsey and Xavier Cugat."

Nickie also tended bar at the General Oglethorpe Hotel on Wilmington Island when that grand old structure developed a somewhat shady reputation under the ownership of the Teamsters Union.

Nickie lived on Wilmington Island for a short while in rooms above The Anchorage nightclub where the Walgreen's is now located beside Johnny Mercer Blvd.

He worked for and became friends with the late Willie Haar, who owned a vast array of property on Tybee including the Red Barn, Brass Rail and Rip Tide bars; Mary Butler's and Christy's restaurants, and the bath house, bowling alley, and carnival. Haar also owned land on the west side of Bull River where the marina is now located.

"He was 'The Man'," says Nickie. "He owned about half of everything along the boardwalk, and he was a

Nickie's Bar still operates under his name on Butler Avenue.

fine person, one of the best I ever knew."

"The Brass Rail had a Surf Room facing the beach which seated more than a thousand people. The Catholic Church held a bazaar there once a year."

All of those businesses except Christy's, which is still standing at the corner of Tybrisa and Strand, have long since disappeared.

It was from Haar that Nickie's brother Benny leased the Rip Tide, which became one of Tybee's most famous bars.

"Willie wouldn't allow dancing there though," according to Nickie. "He wouldn't allow dancing in any of the places he leased to others. Everybody had to go to the Brass Rail to dance. That's the way Willie wanted it."

Doc Wall, who opened Doc's Bar, a still popular watering hole after more than 50 years in operation, befriended Nickie early on, hiring him as a bartender and contributing to two of Nickie's most memorable early experiences on the island.

One day I was standing in front of Doc's when he brought a horse up 16th Street to the bar and said, 'You're going to get on that horse'," Nickie laughs. "I said I don't know how to ride, but he put me on that thing, and I took off down 16th Street. I jumped off just after passing the place where the parking lot office is now and let it go. Doc managed to find the horse later."

Wall was an avid pilot and persuaded Nickie to fly with him in an open-seated bi-plane he kept at Hobbs Field, one of two airfields then operating on Wilmington Island.

"He flew that thing low along Little Tybee, dipping his wings at the birds, and I told him he'd better get my ass back home," says Nickie. "That man really loved to fly. I think he's the pilot who got in trouble flying under the Talmadge Bridge."

Wall was also responsible for getting Benny to give his brother a raise.

"He came into the Rip Tide one day and watched me working for a while, then asked Benny what he was paying me to do what I did," says Nickie. "When Benny told him $35 a week, Doc said you'd better give him a raise. He needs one."

"Doc was a really decent, good man," he says. "His was one of the only bars on the island that did not have any gambling at the time."

"Everybody had gambling in the back room back then, and there were slot machines for a while and then a machine where you put seven nickels in and toy horses ran around a track. If yours won, you got a payoff, but of course if you bet on all seven, you never got all your money back."

"Later, there was a big bingo parlor on 16th Street for a long time which was really nice and drew huge crowds, but the sheriff closed it down saying that it was gambling."

Tybee, which was named Savannah Beach back then (Nickie agrees with many long-time residents who feel it lost a lot of business when its name was changed), was the only place in Georgia you could get a drink on Sunday, he says, noting that only 18 of 129 counties in the state permitted the sale of liquor.

"You couldn't display your liquor bottles behind the bar in the 1940s," he says. "You had to keep them under the bar. It was against the law to pour mixed drinks anywhere in Chatham County."

Despite the law, gambling and liquor sales ran rampant on the island, continuing until dawn at some bars.

Old timers say the island's bar owners dodged the law

through an arrangement with toll bridge operators.

At that time there were three low-lying bridges crossing the Wilmington River, Bull River, and Lazaretto Creek, the latter near where Cafe Loco is now located.

A pair of bridge tenders working 12-hour shifts opened each of the spans for boat traffic by pushing the handles on a turntable attached to massive gears to swing the bridges open.

It was a long and laborious process which kept the tenders busy because the bridges were low and required opening for even small boats at high tide.

"The one at Bull River was so low that a 16-foot boat couldn't get under it at high tide and traffic would really back up when they opened it on Sundays, and that's a fact," says Nickie. "That bridge was under water during the '47 hurricane."

When county or state police headed toward Tybee to raid gambling and after-hours bar operations, the bridge tenders would call ahead to warn bar owners while opening their bridges to delay the police, giving islanders sufficient time to shut down their bars before the authorities arrived.

The cops couldn't understand why they rarely found anything illegal when they finally reached the island.

Although his original pizza and beer shack may seem a

small start, Nickie was soon off and running on a track that would make him the undisputed king, and likely the last, of the big time Tybee bistro operators.

At one time he owned five bars on the island and had 19 liquor licenses in Chatham County, with both sides of the 1500 block of Butler Ave. becoming the linchpin of his business empire.

He created the building at 1502 on the east side, adjacent to the "World Famous" Breakfast Club; the one at 1508, where Skipper's restaurant is now, where Nickie operated a wine-and-cheese shop, and the building now occupied by Cousin Vinnie's Pizza Parlor, where he operated the Shrimp Boat Restaurant.

On the corner, at 1518, he opened a nightclub called Kitten's Corner (now Scandals) in 1970, along with two adjacent buildings around the corner on 16th St., at 22 and 24, which now house a bike shop and beauty salon. In the next block to the south, he built the structure now housing the Mity Tidy Laundromat.

On the west side of Butler he built a store housing "NBC," which stood for Nickie's Beverage Co., where a T-shirt shop now operates next to the Sunrise Cafe.

Along with then-Mayor Jimmy Brown, he also rebuilt the Dragon Palace Chinese restaurant, which previously housed the Mousetrap Bar and is currently occupied by the Sunrise Cafe, after a fire.

On the south side of the Sunrise, where Stone's Throw Away is now situated, he built and operated the Pizza King restaurant, and next to that, at 1513 Butler, he built and operated a 15-cent hamburger restaurant in 1966, before selling and buying it back to establish the current Nickie's Lounge.

Nickie remodeled the building at 1515, where his bail bond office was once located. It now houses the recently opened ABC (Alexander's Beverage Co.), and Nickie can often be seen cashing checks there for islanders.

On the west corner of 16th and Butler, he remodeled what was once the three-story Ocean View Hotel. It now houses Benny's Tybee Tavern. Eddie Pasco operated the Port Royal bar there at one time. Pasco also operated a bar by the same name on River Street in Savannah, one of only two on that street at the time.

Nickie also built the two-story apartment building located behind Benny's.

He caused quite a stir at one of his businesses on Butler when he installed a blinking light out front.

"The police swooped down when some lady called them thinking there was a fire," he chuckles.

Not all of his businesses were relegated to the island's south end, however.

In the 1950s, he opened a plush bar and gambling op-

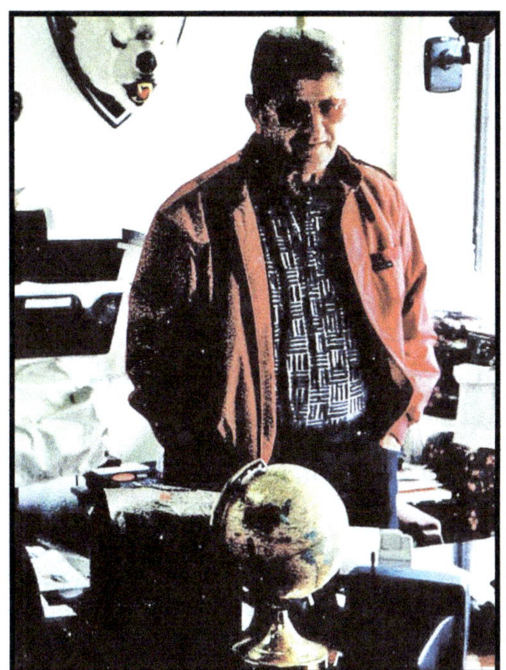
Nickie Alexander in his cluttered bail bond office discussing Tybee enterprises.

eration called the Surf Club that featured blackjack, craps tables, and other forms of gambling on the north end where the Oceanside Nursing Home now stands.

Nickie also had a concession stand at a go-cart track in a field behind the Tybee Lighthouse.

While strip clubs were a regular part of island entertainment at the time, the most famous being The Black Lace Lounge where Cap'n Chris's restaurant is now located, Nickie says he never offered such fare at any of his establishments, although he did have dancing girls in Kitten's Corner at one time.

He solidified his position in the community in the 1970s when he was elected to City Council for two terms.

Interestingly enough, he served as Police Commissioner while on council before Tybee changed to its current city-manager form of government. Nickie still owned three bars on the island at the time.

The police station was then located at the beach end of 16th Street, where the parking lot attendants are now housed. A bigger building was later constructed for both police and a first aid station. That building now houses the Marine Science Center, while the police station was moved to the north end where its holding station had long been located.

Nickie recalls he was talking to Police Chief David McCutchen in front of one of his Butler Ave. businesses in 1962 when the chief got a call asking him to check on a prowler at a house on Lovell Avenue.

Fifteen minutes later, the chief, who was considered by many to be the best in a long line of island police chiefs, was shot through the head and killed.

The occupant of what was thought to be a vacant house shot him through the front door when he approached, apparently thinking McCutchen was the prowler reported earlier. The shooter was never prosecuted.

During his tenure on City Council, Nickie introduced a number of what now seem prescient proposals.

He tried to persuade officials to annex Little Tybee Island and all of the area between Lazaretto Creek and just west of Bull River, including the land where Williams Seafood restaurant once sat.

Nickie visualized the construction of a bridge to Little

Tybee which he hoped would be developed as a recreational area.

"I was disappointed the city didn't do that," he says.

Regarding the other annexation proposal, he says it would have ended the continuing confusion about what belongs to the city and what to the county, "And I still think with this road widening thing you're going to see houses built all along that highway. It would pay off eventually for the city to own all of that."

"And I can't see how anyone can oppose a new road. It's underwater now at extreme high tides just beyond Ft. Pulaski, and thousands of cars use it. Jesus Christ, every high schooler now drives his own car. As long as you 've got that sunshine and water, people are going to come here."

Neither proposal ever came to fruition.

He also tried to persuade the city to build a new concrete-and-steel fishing pier on the site of the old Pavilion at a total cost of $495,000 to be paid for with motel and hotel tax revenues.

"I got approval from the Corps of Engineers, but I couldn't get council to go along with it," he says.

The current pier and Pavilion, built later by Chatham County, has been the subject of controversy in recent years because of what some say is the lack of maintenance and housekeeping on and around the site.

Nickie says, "One of the biggest disappointments of my life is when they eliminated the median strip on Butler Avenue to make it a four-lane highway. Those palm trees lining the median were beautiful! It broke my heart."

He says that in addition to beautifying the road, the palm trees blocked the wind coming from the north which now sweeps down the street, turning over garbage cans and pushing trash in its path.

"Those palm trees on Butler were the biggest asset I've ever seen," says Nickie, who believes the route could still hold four lanes and a median with palms if the present parking along both sides of the street is eliminated.

Nickie's off-island properties included the Crow Bar on Wilmington Island, Alexander's Bonding Co. on U.S. Highway 17, and Nickie's Lounge and Drive-in at 41st and Abercorn in Savannah, where Perry Hubbard's bar was once located.

Perhaps because of his far-flung gambling, bar and bail bonding operations, unsubstantiated rumors have occasionally circulated that Nickie may have connections with the underworld, but he's understandably reluctant to discuss such stories.

"I don't talk about that stuff," he says. Then, grinning, adds: "I might get a couple of calls, one in particular I don't need."

During the last few years Nickie, who is now 84, sold most of his businesses, including the bail bonding office where those huge jars of pennies were displayed. He donated the pennies, which totaled over $4,000 once students finished counting them, to St. Michael's School.

He says he believes the timing of his property sales is about right since he thinks Tybee will become more of a residential retirement community, with far fewer businesses in the future, given the rapid increase in property values.

"If you own a business, like a bar or a restaurant, and someone comes along and says, 'I'll give you a million and a half,' how can you resist? How long would it take you to recover that kind of money working? If you've got over a million dollars, wouldn't someone have trouble selling you a job? When you buy a restaurant or bar to operate, you're buying a job."

Looking back over his years on the island, Nickie says: "It's hard to accept what it's turned into over what it was 40 or 50 years ago. I remember when I used to pick up the phone in the late '40s, and I would call down to the switchboard in a home which is still there next to, the Tybee Market where there were two operators, and I would say, 'Beulah, would you get Willie Haar on the phone for me', and she would say, 'Nickie, he's not

Nickie and Voncyle.

here. He's gone to town for a movie'. That was then."

"And I remember the first piece of property I ever bought down here. It was $350 for a building lot, and that was high then."

Nickie now has a residence in Thunderbolt with Voncyle, his wife of 51 years.

"You know," he says, when he mentions Voncyle, "I really believe it's true, what Dale Carnegie said in his book How to Win Friends and Influence People, about behind ever successful man is a good woman."

Nickie still maintains an island house on Lovell Avenue. It has a neat and what would normally seem welcoming front yard, but a bevy of signs posted near the entrance make it seem far less than inviting.

One on his garage reads "Go Away;" two on his white picket fence warn "Beware, Dog Bites", and one on a post in the yard reads "German Shepherd Drive". Yet another instructs visitors to "Park at Meters Only. Tow Away Zone." That one's a head scratcher since there are no parking meters on Lovell Ave.

Nickie remains a familiar sight driving around Tybee in one of his three vintage Chevrolet El Camino pickup trucks with Frosty, his big white German shepherd, who, while a really lovable animal, is presumably the subject of those dog warning signs, perched in the back.

Nickie's name remains embedded in the sidewalk in front of the bar he opened on Butler Avenue in 1971.

You can still see Nickie's name embedded in the sidewalk on the west side of the 1500 block of Butler. Nearby, in the Park of the Seven Flags at the terminus of Highway 80, you can also find his and Voncyle's names inscribed on a bench he donated to the city.

Nickie Alexander is the last of Tybee's bistro kingpins, and, while he may have lost a step or two over the years, he's certain to leave a huge footprint on the island.

POSTSCRIPT: Nicholas "Nickie" Alexander passed away on March 10, 2016 at his home on Tybee. He was 94. His wife, Voncyle, was 79 when she passed away on July 8, 2013.

Dirty Dan -
The Peanut Man & Much More!

He'll Handle Your Taxes & Tax Your View

Dirty Dan Deloach

How'd you like to have a guy named Dirty Dan do your tax return?

Don't laugh! Tybee's Dan Deloach operates his own accounting firm on Butler Avenue and has an outstanding reputation. He's also a successful real estate investor.

The "Dirty Dan" moniker stems from his former business title: "Dirty Dan, the Peanut Man." The peanut part is not a reference to his munchkin-like appearance (he's just a couple of inches over 5 feet tall in his flip flops). It's the product he was purveying at the time.

After experimenting for two years, Dan started a Savannah company producing frozen boiled peanuts in 1986. The product was not the oxymoron its description suggests.

Those who tried them say they were yummy, and they sold quite well. Much of their success, aside from that good taste, was attributed to the process Dan developed for their uniform configuration and his process for their preparation.

He used the Valencia variety, which has four peanuts to the shell, and his process eliminated "pops," those empty shell segments filled with salt water that leave boiled peanut aficionados feeling cheated.

To ensure uniformity, Dan started his process with dry peanuts rather than the green ones normally used for boiling. He culled the dry ones for pops. There are more dry peanuts than wet ones per pound, so he got more for his money.

During processing the boiled nuts absorbed water, enabling him to sell fewer peanuts per pound than he purchased. Less for more is not a bad business formula.

Another major reason for his company's initial success was Dan's penchant for promotion. He'd visit locations where his peanuts were sold dressed in overalls and a straw hat and pitch his product to customers with amusing, distinctly double-entendre descriptions (he rapped and spouted poems about peas and nuts and, well, you get the picture).

Dan says he had a great time, and customers, particularly women, for whom he has a special affinity, were delighted with his spiel.

He was about to strike it rich when the bubble burst

immediately after he landed a contract with a major supermarket chain for placement of his peanuts in 110 of its grocery stores. A shipment of 400 cases was rejected when the refrigerator system in the truck hauling them broke down causing the cartons to partially collapse.

"The peanuts were fine, but the boxes wouldn't stack properly, and the warehouse manager refused to accept the shipment," Dan says.

His production plant in Savannah had limited frozen storage, and, with 5,000 pounds of fresh peanuts arriving for processing, he couldn't handle the fresh batch and the rejected shipment. The new peanuts sat in boxes for an extended period of time before Dan was ready to process them. By then bugs had gotten to them, and 5,000 pounds of peanuts had to be dumped.

Dan gave up the operation and his dreams of becoming Peanut King of the South but took it in stride saying: "Those things happen in life." He hangs onto the nickname Dirty Dan because he likes it and savors memories of those peanut pitchman days.

He also refers to himself occasionally as a "redneck cracker," but don't be deceived by that self-deprecating depiction. Dan is known for his down-home wit and wisdom, and the peanut operation was one of the rare instances where he didn't come out ahead. He's been known to pinch a penny so hard that Lincoln squeals.

When he was growing up in Savannah, Dan ran around with several buddies, one of whom drove a stylish 12-cylinder Packard. They would pick up attractive female companions and take in a movie.

"We'd buy one box of popcorn to share with the broads," he says. Then they'd buy a loaf of bread and head down to Johnny Harris Restaurant on Victory Drive where they knew one of the cooks.

The boys would get him to make them a 35-cent barbeque sandwich, heaping it with hot sauce, then ask him for some of the ribs that were being discarded. "In those days they didn't sell chipped barbecue, and there were ribbons with plenty of meat left on those bones," says Dan.

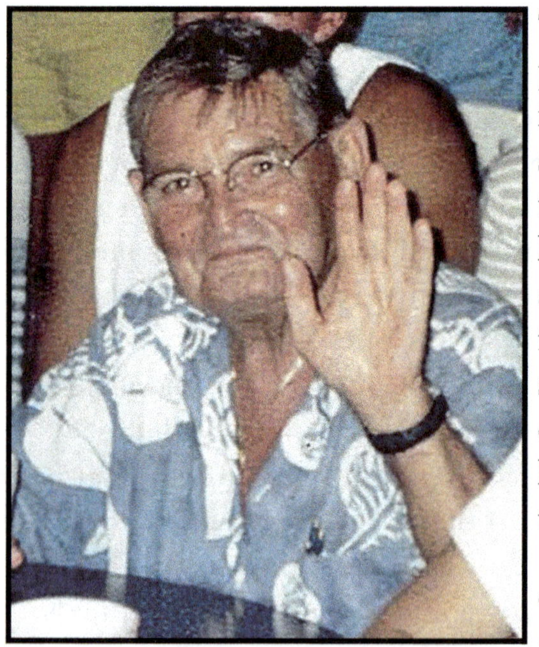

Dan Deloach in a party mood as usual.

The boys would press their bread into the extra hot sauce, then shave off the slivers of meat left on the bones and treat their girlfriends to barbecue sandwiches. They'd cap off the evening by taking the girls to a dance hall.

"We didn't drink in those days, and

we'd get them a seat at the bar and order a Coke, then dare those broads to take more than a sip," Dan laughs. "It'd only be about 11 p.m., and we were going to dance until 2 a.m. We had a ball, and it didn't cost much!"

Dan is a native Savannahian and has always been creative when it comes to making and saving a buck and having fun. At the age of 4 he would climb the fig tree in his back yard and take the figs down the street to sell them. At 6, he earned money shining shoes, and, when he got a little older, he had a couple of newspaper delivery routes and worked as a soda jerk.

Dan joined kids from more affluent families at the posh DeSoto Hotel pool when he was 9 by getting permission to swim in exchange for helping to clean the pool. He picked up extra money in junior high school by learning to be a movie projectionist and running the projector for movies nightly at the USO.

And he worked as a lifeguard at the old DeSoto Beach Hotel on Tybee, after acquiring his Red Cross Water Safety Instructor's certification when he was only 14. The normal 17-year-old age requirement for certification was dropped during World War II when most young men were away in the service.

Dan hitchhiked out to the beach each day for that job. "I never had any trouble getting out," he says. "If you couldn't hitch a ride in less than three minutes back then, something was wrong."

But that endless throng of pretty girls at the pool proved to be his first financial downfall. Between the newspaper routes, movie projection, and life guarding, Dan was earning almost $100 a week, tax free, which was great money in those days. By the time he was 16 he had socked away $3,000.

"That disappeared in a summer," he laughs. "Between taking flying lessons and the women, and I spent more on them than the lessons, I was broke when I turned 17."

Dan's summers seemed endless, and Tybee was the place to be. "One of the good things about it then was that if you got a little drunk or in a little trouble, any of the 'normal' stuff, the police chief would just lock you up overnight," says Dan. "He wouldn't book you, just lock you up, and you could tell your folks you just decided to stay at the beach that night. Tybee was fun then. They've taken that away."

Occasionally, Dan would take a break from the lifeguard stand to join other teenagers at the beach for outings in their parents' expensive boats. He returned home after one of those excursions to inform his mother that he wanted one of those flashy boats.

"We can't afford a boat," he recalls his mother responding. "We don't have an automobile. Your sister doesn't have a bicycle. We're poor."

"I didn't know we were poor," he laughs. "I'd of never

known we were poor if my Mamma hadn't told me."

His father had left his family's farm in Bullock County in the 1920s when he married and moved to Savannah where he drove street cars and read electric meters. But his dad knew a thing or two about investing.

When they moved to Savannah he purchased a duplex, renting out one side so tenants helped pay the mortgage. It got them through the Depression, and he told his son to follow the duplex approach when he grew up.

Dan says he still follows that advice in real estate investments because "it's the smart thing to do. Let the other man create your wealth."

But he admits he wasn't much of a scholar in his days at Savannah High School. "I was kicked out of Savannah High, so I went off to Georgia Military College."

"I went to college quite a bit," he chuckles. "I played a lot of bridge at Armstrong College when I was 16 to 18. My name is Daniel David Deloach, and I majored in D's. Every subject I took was a D."

He dropped out to join the Navy during the Korean War. "One of the most stimulating tours I had in the Navy was in Venice and Lido, an island just off of Venice," says Dan.

He discovered an outdoor concert on Lido where 150 musicians were playing for free. "They were playing the William Tell Overture when I walked up, and I just sat there for two hours enjoying the music. I wonder why they can't have something like that down on River Street."

Navy service was another good deal for Dan. "I was on the USS Coral Sea, and all we did was visit Grecian islands, Italy, and Paris," he says. "I fought the battle of the prostitutes on the French Riviera. The toughest part of my tour was coming back to Norfolk, Virginia, in the winter."

After his discharge he wanted to take advantage of the G.I. Bill but felt he wasn't equipped for college. Bridge, not scholarship, had been his strong suit.

One night an ex-G.I. friend who was attending Armstrong gave him a ride that changed his life. It was a school night, and Dan asked his buddy why he wasn't in class. His friend explained that he had four years of free schooling under the G.I. Bill, and, if he attended all his classes, he might pass. Since Armstrong was only a two-year school at the time, he had to fail some classes to utilize all the free schooling.

"This is for me," Dan concluded, noting: "I'm serious as a heart attack." It was at Armstrong that he discovered it was not his intellect but his disdain for study which had hampered his scholarship. "I had just never cracked a book," he laughs.

By chance, he enrolled in an accounting class, not even

knowing what accountants did. During the first session of that class the professor described the unlimited employment opportunities available to accountants since every business needs one and everybody needs a tax person. Every salesclerk is a part of accounting and every guy working in a stock room, the professor said.

That struck a chord which still resounds for Dan. "I propped myself up in bed that night with a drink, and for the first time since the sixth grade I looked at a book," he says. "I read everything in that book, and by the time I went to sleep I had completed six assignments.

"During the next class session I heard these smart guys asking the dumbest damned questions, and I realized I was actually studying. Accounting was a natural for me."

After graduation he got a job in Atlanta with the income tax section of the State Revenue Department, working his way up from a file clerk to field auditor. Shortly after being transferred to Savannah, he resigned to open his own accounting office.

He struggled for a while but got a break when he was asked to teach an accounting class at Bowlen-Draughn Business College, predecessor of South College, which supplemented his income until he built up his clientele.

Dan says he got to know Mills B. Lane, former head of the C&S Bank, while he was in Savannah. "He was a bum," says Dan, but he means it in a complimentary way. "He'd go out and walk the streets early in the morning, without a shave and wearing a Colombo-type trench coat even in the summer."

Lane was wealthy and could have lived anywhere but he chose to live downtown. "He wasn't one of those social climbers or society bugs. I'm not saying there's anything wrong with those, but it ain't my type of style. And Mills Lane wasn't like that. He had his share of finery and things like that, but he also ran from it." That's what Dan means when he says: "He was a bum!"

Dan got started in real estate investment shortly after his accounting business took off, and it became the main contributor to his financial success. He got in on the ground floor in the 1960s, before the development of Historic Savannah.

One of his first purchases was a four-story building on Liberty Street near the DeSoto Hotel into which he moved his business offices. "Back then," he says, "you could go to one bank and borrow $500 for a down payment, then go to another to finance the mortgage. And houses on Gaston and Barnard Streets were selling for $3,500."

Dan thrived on that formula. He bought one large house for $10,900 and sold it for $110,000. "It was good to me," he says of that venture.

Dan left his accounting business in Savannah in the 1970s "because it just got to be too much of a headache for me in those days."

He purchased a house on Wilmington Island where he moved and opened an office. Dan laughs when he recalls buying that property.

"My wife wanted the ocean, and I wanted the river," he says. "My pocketbook had me settle on the marsh." Dan initially paid $5,500 for the property, which he describes as breathtaking.

"When you get either a new or a full moon along with a northeaster covering the marsh with water, it's the most beautiful view I've ever seen," he says. "That house must have been built in the dead of winter. You look directly into the new moon on Dec. 21." He has refused an offer of $160,000 for the property.

After working on Wilmington for a while Dan found that most of his clients lived on Tybee, so he purchased property there, moving out in 1992.

"Besides," he says, "I loved dancing, and I love the DeSoto, and I figured I could get a little drunk and I could still get home."

Dan purchased the building which houses his business and other rental property on Tybee, but he still lives frugally, sleeping on a couch in his office. "Heck, I used to go to sleep watching TV on the couch in the Wilm-

Dirty Dan Deloach parties with Sylvia Gott (see Chapter 20) at Doc's Bar

ington house," he laughs. "What's the difference?"

Recently, he bought a huge touring bus that had been meticulously converted to a recreational vehicle. He plans to spend some time on it in Florida's keys. "I love Tybee," he says "but I like to travel. The Keys to me are similar to Tybee, only in the Keys the city officials know people like to have fun, and they support community businesses."

"If a guy there's not causing any trouble, if he staggers, they say give him another drink. I love their attitude. It's a way of life where you do what you want as long as you don't harass or intimidate anyone."

"Tybee Island's not that way. It could be a fun place to come, and then people would get a room (after partying all evening) rather than driving back."

Still, Dan feels Tybee's real estate is one of the best bargains on the East Coast. He'd like to hold onto his office and find the right person to run it for him while he works out of the big RV, staying in touch with the office by phone and computer.

He'll be taking a female companion along on his trips, of course. Dan remains very much attracted to the ladies.

"I like the old broads," he says. "You take a young one, and you can rub your hand over that tight skin real quick. But you take an old, wrinkled one, and you can take your time and make all kinds of patterns and designs on those wrinkles."

Dan made another sweet deal on the bus purchase. "Those things are selling for $150,000 to $200,000," he says. You don't even want to know what he paid for it.

Dirty Dan's now 68 and he's still on a roll.

POSTSCRIPT: The City of Tybee honored Dan with the keys to the City on his 80th birthday declaring January 8, 2009, as Dirty Dan Day. He passed away at 85 on August 19, 2014. Memorial services celebrating Dan's life, including tall tales, beach music, and the distribution of his colorful old beach shirts were attended by hundreds of his friends on September 17, 2014, in the former Marlin Monroe's Surfside Grill on Tybee. One of his

flower-bedecked beach shirts still hangs on a door in my beach house.

George McDonald -
Famous Folks? She Knew 'em!

Looking Forward
While
Glancing Back

She shot marbles with Johnny Mercer. She attended Juliette Gordon Low's first Girl Scouts session. She cuddled Chatham Superior Court Judge George Oliver when he was a baby. She has cavorted on Tybee Island for nearly 100 years.

And George McDonald - that's right, George ("It just fell on my shoulders since there were already two girls," she says. "My daddy had given up on having a boy.") - is looking forward enthusiastically to the turn of another century.

"Oh, my!" she exclaims. "Think of that! The year 2000! Who would believe it!"

George celebrated her 94th birthday in October, and name notwithstanding, is every inch a lady who sparkles with energy, charm, and wit. "Actually, it was a real advantage," she says of her name. "At the start of every school year, I was always seated on the boys' row, and I didn't mind that. I liked the boys!"

George lives on Tybee with her younger sister, Caroline, who celebrated her 88th birthday Dec. 14. Their home is delightfully decked for the holidays and Caroline's birthday with numerous pots of poinsettias provided by Oelschig Nursery in Savannah, the owners of which they have known since they were children. "They never forget me," smiles George. "They keep us in flowers year-round."

Her father worked for the railroad, and the family moved to the beach on May 1 each year. "May Day was always Tybee Day, and we'd come down on the train," she recalls. "I wasn't introduced to the island. It was introduced to me in 1903!"

George and her family lived near Wesleyan College ("Chiang Kai-Shek's girls went there, you know!" she says) in Macon through her grade school days, then moved to Savannah, but their traditional Tybee excursions continued through the years.

"Since my dad worked for the railroad, we had passes to ride, and it was always great fun." she recalls. "The engineer would stop at Cockspur Island on the way out and let us pick blackberries."

"And the good kids - those who didn't open windows on the trip out (letting ash from the coal burning locomotive into passenger cars) - were allowed to ride with the engineer while the engine was rotated on the turntable (at the south end of Tybee near Inlet and Chatham Avenue) for the return back to Savannah."

George admits that she was not always one of the "good kids," but received preferential treatment because of her father's profession.

Even after the train's demise, when the road to the beach was completed (George watched from the train window as the road was built with dirt dredged from the Savannah River's South Channel), the family's annual island pilgrimage continued.

"It was exciting to have the highway come through," she says. "We drove out in a huge Studebaker we called 'the hearse' because it looked like one."

Her father traded "the hearse" in on a smaller open-air Studebaker when she was old enough to drive, because "he said it didn't look lady-like for me to drive that big old car," says George, whose family lived in several houses in Savannah.

"My daddy used to say we moved so much that when Mother went out in the yard to feed the chickens they turned over on their backs," she laughs. "Mother said they thought we were moving again since she used to tie their feet to move them."

George became friends with some of Savannah's most famous residents during her teen years. Her family lived near Charlton and Lincoln streets, just behind the Cathedral, when Juliette Gordon Low moved into a house on the square in front of it.

Low came over from England where she had started a group called the Girl Guides and wanted to form an organization with the same name here, "but that name didn't sound American enough for us," says George.

Ultimately the group settled on the name Girl Scouts, and George joined the first troop, which held meetings in a carriage house behind the Low residence. "She was a wonderful lady, and she made a lady out of me," says George, who joined the Scouts when she was 12 and has remained a member for 82 years.

Girl Scouts flock to her home on Tybee when they learn that she knew the founder of their organization. George says Low always brought a small hammer with her when she came to fish on Tybee and would hit those she caught "to put them out of their misery."

The Girl Scout's founder was not the only famous person George rubbed shoulders with while growing up in Savannah. She played marbles with Johnny Mercer when he was a young boy.

"We were hard on him because he was the scrappiest little nothing you've ever seen," she says. "He'd run and tell his Aunt Annie everything we did."

"We rapped his knuckles all the time because he cheated. He'd shoot a marble out of the ring, and, when he thought no one was looking, he'd amble over and kick it closer. That's when we'd rap his knuckles, and he'd run home to tell his aunt."

Later, Mercer attended dances at George's home. "We really loved to dance in those days," she says. "As teenagers we would have 'pound parties' on Friday nights, inviting our friends to bring a pound of something, like fruit or anything else, to eat. Johnny was always the first one there because he knew there'd be something to eat."

George says Mercer's talents were recognized when he was sent to a military school in Milledgeville and became quite popular there entertaining at parties when students learned he could play the piano. "Then he wrote 'Moon River' and that started him on his way," she says. "We were all just delighted when he got into the movies."

She has known Judge Oliver - who handled the first three trials of Jim Williams, the central figure in the book and movie "Midnight in the Garden of Good and Evil" – "since he was in diapers and knee pants," she says.

"He lived across the street from us in Savannah with two maiden aunts. He was much younger than us, but he was a wonderful boy, and he's a wonderful guy. He's doing fine."

The judge wasn't always an angel, however, according to her sister Caroline. "I remember when his aunts used to jerk him up and pop him and say, 'Get in this house!' and he'd say, 'Well, dammit I guess I'd better go,'" she laughs. "He was only about 10 at the time.

But he's really a fine man and a fine judge."

Speaking of "The Book," Caroline says "everybody thinks that book is just such a great deal for Savannah, but I think it's one of the most horrendous things that has ever happened."

"It made us look like thugs, but gosh, the money he's (John Berendt) made on it! The power of that book! You meet somebody from St. Louis, and they'll say 'Oh, you're from that town that has The Book,' and I'll say we had a town before that book was ever conceived on that boy's stupid brain!"

Caroline says she read the book until she got to the "voodoo, hoodoo part and I skipped over that. I'm an avid reader, good, bad, or indifferent, but that wasn't even bad enough or indifferent enough."

George's face becomes radiant when she remembers the big-band dances she attended on the old Tybee Pavilion as a teenager. "When I walk out on that new Pavilion, I wish I could record what's going on in my mind," she says. "The years just roll back. I used to dance my soul away on the old Pavilion."

She liked dancing with older boys since she felt those her own age were "silly, mamma's boys," and recalls swaying to the big-band sounds of Fred Waring, Guy Lombardo, and Bennie Goodman.

George and her friends felt safe because "our parents

were always nearby keeping a watch on us," she says. "They saw to it that we didn't wander off among the dunes when the moon was rising!"

While her parents had strict rules about fraternizing with soldiers from Fort Screven, she still managed to sneak away for afternoon walks on the beach with some of them. "That was exciting because we thought we were getting away with something, but we never did anything," she smiles, confessing, however, that sometimes they hid in the dunes "to smooch a little."

"Every spring a new crop would come down," she laughs, "and we didn't miss much. But our parents saw that we went with the right people, and they allowed us to bring them home to dance."

She also recalls watching the Rev. Burke Day baptize people in the ocean. Day was the founder of the Days Inn motel chain, the first of which was built on Tybee. "It was a regular showtime on Easter Sundays when he would baptize six to ten people," she says. "They'd have to wait there until the tide was right."

She weathered the hurricane of 1918 in a summer house at the beach end of Izlar Avenue. George says no one knew anything was about to happen at the time, and her mother had gone to town with visiting friends, leaving her and another teenage girl alone in their beach house.

"When we got the warning, there was a lot of beach,

with the tide far out, and we moved everything out of the house to the beach. That's how much sense we had!"

All of their household goods were quickly covered by the windblown tidal surge while the girls hunkered down in the house, but, once the storm passed and the water receded, George says she and her friend found everything on the beach and dragged it back to the house.

After completing high school in Savannah, George received her degree in home economics at the University of Georgia, then earned her master's degree in Statesboro. She taught home economics, mostly at Chatham Junior High School in Savannah, for 39 years.

Her mother, Matthew Louise Wagner (George figures she was named for "some evangelist") started the first school lunch program in Chatham County. "During World War II, she started a soup kitchen in the basement of the old Chatham Academy for less fortunate people in the area," says George.

"Out of that came the suggestion to open a school lunchroom to provide children with soup and sandwiches. That's where the school lunch program came from." Not long afterward, her mother opened another lunch program, working with the PTA, at a new junior high school on Bull Street. The program was called Mrs. Wagner's Lunchroom, and her mother remained active in it for years.

George stopped teaching at age 26, when she met and married Ryan McDonald. "Mac filled both of my eyes," she smiles. "I couldn't see anything else but him, and I trapped him."

She won't disclose how, because "that's a secret a lady doesn't tell."

She traveled extensively with Mac, who was auditor for a biscuit company with offices throughout the mid-Atlantic states and New England, until they settled on Long Island for four years. On one of her first trips to New York City, she was delighted when she found Fred Waring, who she remembered from those dances on Tybee, playing at the Pennsylvania Hotel.

When Mac took early retirement due to illness, they returned to Savannah, where George resumed her teaching career. She wanted to include boys in her home economics classes, "but they couldn't stand that," she says.

"By that time, John Rousakis had grown big enough to be the mayor, and I told him that men were now staying at home, and their wives were working to support 'em. They've got to have home economics. You don't want them to grow up like you, do you?"

When Rousakis expressed little interest in her plan, she reminded him of the time when, as a mischievous junior-high student, he sneaked into her class and mixed Dutch Cleanser with canisters containing sugar and flour.

"It was against the law to hit anybody at the time, but, boy, if looks and words could have done the job, they'd have fired me," she laughs.

It wasn't long before her husband Mac became restless from sitting around the house, and George was panic stricken one day when she returned home from her classes, and he wasn't there.

George McDonald gets ready to fire up her stove with dried pine cones to make Hoppin' John.

"Just like a wife would do, I looked through all the closets to see if his clothes were gone," she says. "I thought he had just jumped up and left." She fretted about Mac's whereabouts until late in the evening, then became gripped with fear, convinced it would be bad news, when someone knocked at the door.

When she opened the door, there was Mac, "grinning from ear to ear." He had read about an accounting job at a dairy company just down the street from their house and had gone out to apply.

When the dairy owner heard Mac's qualifications, he put him to work immediately, says George. "Mac was still wearing his coat and hat!"

"I was so mad I could have killed him for scaring me," she recalls. "I kept my bedroom door locked that night, but I fixed his breakfast the next morning because I didn't want him breaking any dishes."

George says Mac was a genius with figures. He would sit across the table from her while she struggled to add columns of numbers for her monthly attendance report, finally looking at the columns, which were upside down from his position, and give her the totals. "He'd rather do that than correct my mistakes," she laughs.

Her husband worked at the dairy farm for several years, with George meeting him at the office each day after school. One day she had an odd premonition and came directly home rather than stopping at his office.

Mac was there, dead from a heart attack. He was 59.

That was more than 40 years ago. George never remarried. "You know I get angry sometimes about being left alone for all these years," she says. "But God and His ways work. Every time I begin to get mad at God, I think about people who become invalids or suffer from mental illness and live for years. That would be terrible."

George, who feels she is blessed with good health, says neither she nor her sister have ever had a drink containing alcohol. "I think our father would have scalped us before day," she laughs. "We didn't have it and we didn't need it. We grew up with others who did, but we were having a wonderful time. We weren't sissies by any means, but our parents were always in the background, and we didn't mind that."

George moved to Tybee, where she remains active in community affairs and continues "doing the things I want to do" after retiring in her late 60s.

She was a founder of the Tybee Lighthouse Museum at Fort Screven in the 1980s. "Nobody wanted it at the time," she recalls. "People said nobody would go there. They said the roof leaked, and you'd get water up to your knees when it rained, and in the winter, you'd freeze and, in the summer, you'd sweat to death and exhibits would mildew."

George persevered, however, becoming friends with

George McDonald, left, with her sister, Caroline.

Adele Fleetwood, who she says, "was very influential here. She had a lot of money and told me her husband was spending a lot, and she wanted to spend some of it."

"It's the only true Georgia museum in the state," she claims. "We don't have anything but Georgia stuff in there." George remained on the museum board of directors until a few years ago.

She continued driving until she reached the age of 90 and was told her license couldn't be renewed. "I was honest about it even though I knew a lot of people were still driving at 94 and older," she says. "I didn't tell anybody, but I wouldn't ride with them either. I said the law says you're not capable, so I'm not going to trust you!"

Her main lament about not driving anymore is the need to depend on others to go places, particularly to church on Sunday mornings. "It was difficult getting accustomed to waiting for somebody to pick you up," she says.

George attends Trinity Chapel United Methodist Church on the island, and says she grew up as a Methodist, but returned to that church only after Mac passed away. "I was a Methodist, and he was a Baptist, but I sure as hell wasn't going to join the Baptist church," she laughs. "I wouldn't be dipped!" They compromised by joining the Presbyterian church.

Despite her influence and wide circle of friends, George says she has never had any desire to enter politics on Tybee. "There's too many dirty crooks down here," she says. "They were born on Tybee and sometimes I think they were laid in a nest of turtle eggs. Crooked? Oh, God, they're crooked. Past masters! I'd have some of them buried so deep they'd never crawl out."

She is particularly perturbed by what she feels is the lukewarm response by Tybee's elected officials to the proposals for Tybrisa Street prepared recently by SCAD students as an extended class project. "I want to help these kids from SCAD. Their plans are an idea aborning, but so many people have wanted to change the street that it's just a thought in the breeze."

"Tybrisa has a reputation for cheap bars and ladies of the dark. They look at that area, and it's so desolate and hopeless that they turn away, without doing anything about it."

Her own preference is to have the street closed to traffic and turned into a mall between Butler Avenue and the Pavilion, and that will be one of her principal goals for the new year. "I hope Mrs. Day (mother of State Rep. Burke Day Jr.) can work hard enough to bring it about," says George. "She might be able to do it."

But George's immediate priority is New Year's Day, when she plans to cook up her traditional batch of Hoppin' John on an old wood-burning stove in her kitchen. She has dried pinecones in window boxes throughout the year to use for fuel "when I fire it up!"

The old stove, which serves as an ornament most of the time, comes in handy on other occasions as well. "When the electricity goes off on the island, I'm the only one who can brew up a cup of coffee!" she proclaims with pride.

George says she is making no long-range plans and lives by the motto "Come day, go day, God send Sunday," but she is looking forward to the 21st century with considerable excitement.

"It's just two years away!" George grins. "Oh, my. Just imagine that!"

***POSTSCRIPT:** Sadly, George McDonald failed to greet the new century she had looked forward to with such enthusiasm. She passed away on July 29, 1998. The house where she kept her old pine-cone-burning stove is now operated as the Bluebird Bed & Breakfast.*

John O'Neill -
A Man of Many Means

Meet an Original Tybee Beach Bum

John O'Neill wound up that way after doing a couple of other things. His employment background lends new meaning to the term "diversification." This "bum" has had careers in radio, television, public relations, personnel, the restaurant business, and as a car salesman, musician, and police officer for two cities.

His last police position ended somewhat abruptly after John was on a streak. Well, streaking is what it was!

John, then a Savannah cop, was attending a police seminar in Statesboro, and was housed in a dormitory at Georgia Southern College when it happened. Always an adventuresome sort, he decided to go out on the town following one of those hum-drum afternoon sessions.

John used a police car for transportation, not his own, but a state trooper's car that happened to be parked right there - with the keys in it! He was extraordinarily thirsty after all that cop shop talk, and it turned out to be quite a night just trying to innocently quench his thirst.

One of the evening's "happenings" occurred when John returned the trooper's car in the wee morning hours and a young lady, who just happened to be riding with him, decided to join a pair of coed friends who were out for late night exercise, jogging about the campus.

Since they seemed to be enjoying the fresh air sans clothing, she doffed her apparel and dashed off to streak with them. That seemed like a good idea to John, and, since the girls were heading toward his dormitory anyway, he joined them in his own birthday suit.

A small problem developed after he streaked into the dorm with them and discovered it was not his, but an adjacent dormitory which housed coeds. He made record time in his sprint down the hall, out the far exit, and back to his own building.

Given that the place was swarming with cops, there was a big-time investigation of the incident. But no one was identified, and no charges were filed. While relieved, John was just a trifle disappointed that he never even got a phone call from any of the young ladies who witnessed his romp. "That ought to tell you something," he laughs, recalling the event.

Campus officials and police kept a tight lid on the escapade, and nothing was ever printed in the media. Until now.

John quietly resigned his position with the Savannah Police Department shortly after informing his superiors of his role in the streaking incident. "Of all the things I've done, that's the one I'll likely be remembered for," John chuckles.

He spends a lot of time nowadays at the DeSoto Beach Hotel's Shipwatch Lounge where he serves as the drummer on weekends with Rick and Debbie's NX Change Band. It was at this DeSoto bar where the bumming thing all began.

It was at one of their foggier late-night soirees that John and a bunch of other island imbibers decided to form a losing softball team. "Losing" was the operable word since the group vowed not to play to win but just to have fun in another whistle-wetting environment.

They frustrated opposing teams by lying about the field sipping brews while fly balls sailed over their heads. They did have a lot of fun, and, somewhat inadvertently, they actually won a game, the final one of the season, after leveling the playing field by plying their opponents with beer prior to the game.

This was obviously a cause for celebration, as almost anything was for this group which adopted, quite appropriately, the name "Beach Bums." Their proposed celebration grew with each sip from the keg, and they wound up with a real extravaganza which included a

homecoming parade, awards ceremony, and homecoming dance.
It was that homecoming parade, during which the group stumbled from the beach at 16th Street back to the DeSoto that initiated the now-popular annual Beach Bum Parade which draws thousands to Tybee every year.

John and other members of the original Beach Bums ball team have given up softball as too much work, even with the relaxed approach they brought to the field, but they are still active in staging the big parade.

Bumming and banging the drums is not the only thing John does, however. He and his wife, Judy, are the successful owners and operators of a real estate company on Tybee. They met while John was still an island cop and Judy encouraged him to shed his police uniform, but this time not to streak.

"Isn't it time you got yourself a real job?" John quotes Judy as asking.

As is often the case, he took her advice, settling into a more traditional breadwinner's role by becoming regional public relations representative for Memorial Medical Center where he remained for seven years before joining Judy in opening the real estate firm.

John is originally from Savannah but spent much of his youth, as did Judy, at their respective parents' beach houses. John did spend one year away from

Savannah during the seventh grade, attending a small school in Maryland where he learned to play the drums and managed to anchor his education.

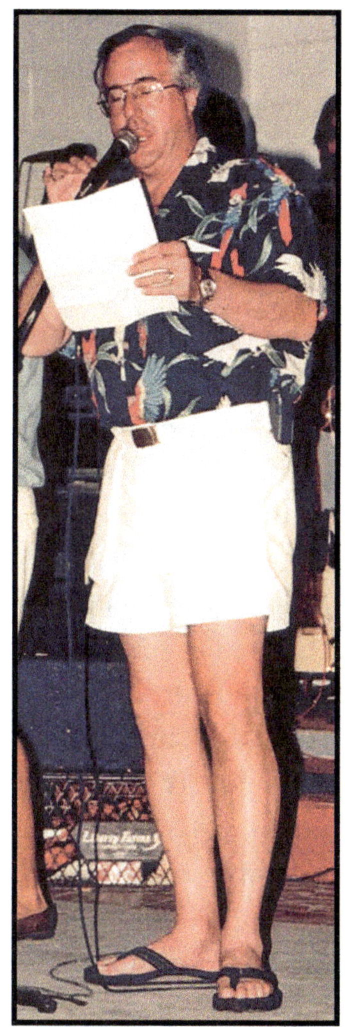

John O'Neill serving as MC at DeSoto's Sunday talent contest.

"There were only six of us in the class and I learned enough in that year to get me all the way through high school," John claims. "After that I never had to crack a book in school again."

As a teenager he stumbled into his first real job, as he later did many others. John and a buddy had been out on the town when they discovered they didn't have the money to catch the bus back home. The buddy knew Jim Squire, who was working late as a disc jockey at WBYG and figured he would give them a ride home so they walked over to the station.

John, who had spent some time playing the drums with local bands, poked around the place while waiting for the disc jockey to get off. After chatting with some of the staff, he concluded that being a radio personality looked like a fun thing to do.

Squire left the station shortly thereafter to join WSAV, and John was offered the job as disc jockey. John, still in high school at the time, worked there briefly before being employed by WSGA as a DJ handling the 7 to 9 p.m. show when the station reformatted to rock music.

From there, he moved to WTOC (now WCHY), again by happenstance, after he stopped by the station one day to deliver an advertising tape. The news director urged John to join the station, luring him by pointing out that his station had television as well as AM-FM radio.

John served as the DJ for the big band night show there and got his first exposure on television because of another unplanned event. The weatherman for the station's TV broadcasts pre-recorded the 11 p.m. weather segment at 6 p.m. in those days, and the tape for the late show was lost one night, with the weatherman nowhere to be found.

In desperation, the news director grabbed John after his radio spot, dressed him in an old jacket and tie they found in a studio closet, and put him on-air live to cover the weather segment. "I was so scared I don't even remember doing that show at all," laughs John.

He apparently did a pretty good job since the station placed him in its 11 p.m. television weather slot after that. They also moved him to the afternoon radio news broadcast and had him handle the audio for the 6 p.m. TV show.

John left WTOC in 1972 to join the Savannah Police Department, having become enamored of police work while employed as a part-time attendant with a Savannah ambulance service when he was still employed in radio news.

He says it was the chatter of police talk on the ambulance radio, sprinkled with news of what was happening on the street, that first attracted him. John was immediately successful. He was named rookie of the year and wound up in the detective division before being lured back to broadcast television with an offer to anchor the 11 p.m. news on WJCL.

He left the news anchor slot to join "The Pieces of April", a popular local band, while also performing with "The Odd Five", a four-piece house band that played at the Foundation Club. When those bands' gigs petered out, John sold cars for a while, then worked in personnel placement for Republic Personnel before opting for a complete change of careers.

John was employed as assistant manager of one of Carey Hilliard's restaurants after the simple act of eating introduced him to the business. While with WJCL he regularly ad-libbed a live commercial during his news show. The commercial consisted of John munching food on camera brought in from Hilliard's restaurant while telling his audience how great the food was.

"We had one of the first microwaves at the station, and they would heat up the meal just before the commercial," John recalls. "The food would be steaming when we went on air, and it looked delicious. People apparently got hungry just watching me and started crowding into Hilliard's restaurant."

Hilliard liked John's work so much he offered him the job as assistant manager of one of his restaurants. It was at Hilliard's that John met Judy, but, while they were immediately attracted to one another, they got off to a rocky start.

Albeit legally separated, John was still wearing his wedding ring and had forgotten about it when he asked his future wife out for a boat ride. "She looked at my ring finger and said she thought such a date would be 'real cozy with me, you, and your wife'," says John. "I was still trying to explain when she left."

Judy did take the time to listen to John's explanation during a subsequent visit and they finally got together. "One of the things that attracted her to me was the fact that she was living on Tybee, and I was willing to drive out to pick her up for dates," laughs John.

They married on the same day John's divorce became final.

After working at four different Hilliard's locations, during his employment with the chain, he was hired as manager of a McDonald's on Hilton Head. John says, "that place was too big and you had to drive too far to get to and from work."

This prompted him to move to Tybee, where he became a policeman once more in 1980, remaining in that job for two years, until his campus romp and Judy's urging led to the public relations job with Memorial.

After moving to Tybee, John ran for City Council several times before finally being elected in 1987, only to be unsuccessful in several subsequent attempts at re-election. Undaunted, he says he plans to run again in next year's election.

"I'm going for the record if I don't already have it," he laughs. "The most times running for office on Tybee and not being elected." But he takes work on the council quite seriously. When he was a councilman, he refused to use a telephone answering machine because he felt obligated to answer all calls from his constituents in person.

John O'Neill makes a point at City Council meeting.

Like long-time Councilman Jack Youmans, John was known for "telling it like it is" and doing what he felt was best for island residents without catering to pressure groups.

Meanwhile, the drummer's spot with the NX Change Band - another job he acquired by happenstance - keeps John loose these days. "I kept entering the weekly talent contest," John recalls. "I went back time after time, year after year, singing stuff like 'Mac the Knife.' I think the best I ever did was a third place. I've got a terrible voice."

John says the band finally offered him the job as drummer "if I'd just stop singing in the talent contest." He feels he came out way ahead because "I can drink and play and I get paid for it now."

Being a beach bum and entertaining while relaxing over drinks at the DeSoto is about as good as it gets on the island. It's been a circuitous route, but John's finally got it all.

POSTSCRIPT: Although both the NX Change Band and the DeSoto Beach Hotel have now disappeared, John O'Neill has become a beloved fixture on Tybee. He is constantly called upon to emcee events and has become a regular extra in the numerous movies now being filmed in the area.

Sally Bostwick -
Popular Island Artist on a Roll

Now Painting The Things She Prefers

She was a popular area artist for decades, and long-time admirers, along with a host of new ones, are delighted to learn that she's back - with an acrylic flurry.

Sally Bostwick, whose realistic paintings of seaside scenes enthralled thousands from the early 1960s through the late 1980s, a period in which she became known as the "Peoples Painter," put her palette aside for more than 10 years prior to her recent resurgence in the now burgeoning area art movement.

Her return - after the extended hiatus to raise four children and take a respite from her formerly frenzied art activities - got a jump start late last year at the annual Tybee Festival of the Arts held on the Pavilion under the sponsorship of the city and Tybee Arts Association.

When Sally strolled away from that show with more than $6,000 in art sales, she was off and running. Sally was recently named "Artist of the Month" by the arts association in honor of her outstanding work.

One association official, Debbie Robinson, who is also a popular island painter, couldn't be happier for her fellow artist. Debbie says it was Sally's work she most admired when she was a child, and it was the beauty of Sally's paintings that initially inspired her to lay oil on canvas.

Debbie disclosed that for years she attempted to acquire some of Sally's work, but it was only recently, with her return to production, that she was able to purchase a Bostwick painting.

Now, despite the fact that Sally displays her work in her home on a little-traveled section of Tybee's South Campbell Avenue and disdains the use of telephones (she has none in her house), her sales are so brisk that she has trouble maintaining an inventory, even though she paints daily.

Sally's house sports a breathtaking view of the marsh from her rear deck and the windows of the breakfast nook adjoining the kitchen where she works.

Sally, who is as comfortable to be with as your favorite pair of well-worn bedroom slippers, is not a stranger to fame. Her work sold like Tybee's World Famous Breakfast Club omelets in the 60s and 70s at AR Galleries on Savannah's River Street. It was also displayed and had brisk sales at a number of East Coast and European art houses.

During that time she was dubbed the "People's Painter" because everyone could understand and identify with her realistic work and most could afford to purchase it. "I like for people to have original work in their homes and love knowing it's mine," she says. "If nobody buys, what have you gained?"

Longtime Savannah Morning News art critic Marshall L. Reed praised her work during an exhibit at AR Galleries in 1974, noting that both her reputation and voluminous sales were "well deserved."

He described one of her small oils as "an indigo-mooded sunburst with pre-storm clouds" and the "composition is superb." Of her work in a 1972 exhibit, he said

Sally looks over the marsh from the deck behind her home studio.

her scenes of "dunes and moss and surf and seaside are among the finest done anywhere." His only criticism was "that this artist's prices are altogether too modest."

Sally looks back on those days and smiles in agreement with Reed's observation. "Back then if I got $150 for a painting, I thought I'd struck it rich," she laughs. Some of her current work sells for 10 times that amount.

In her early days on Tybee, where she has resided for almost 50 years after moving out from Savannah, Sally operated a studio on Butler Avenue at the site of what is now a bicycle shop, but she gave that up to spend more time with her children.

The studio, where she painted, sold her work, and conducted art classes, was somewhat stressful since Sally prefers seclusion.

Her nearest neighbors - there are none for some distance on either side of her house - are two of her now grown children who live down and across the street from her.

Sally refuses to own or drive an automobile and simply calls on one of her children if she needs something in town. They also field her phone calls at their houses and amble over to deliver her messages.

Large herons and other birds converge on a tidal pond

Sally Bostwick describes some of her paintings in her studio.

off the creek behind her house each day, and a boisterous bevy of raccoons cavort across her deck each night.

One of her favorite pastimes is relaxing on the deck when storm clouds gather to watch the bumper-to-bumper traffic along US 80 in the distance as beachgoers make their arduous exit from the island.

Sally is a naturalist at heart, as was her father who was a surveyor and kept daily journals describing his field trips. Sally still keeps a treasured set of those journals dating back to the early part of the century in a small library in her home.

One of her pet peeves is dabbling artists who paint birds and other wildlife while having little knowledge about them. "You have to know all about a bird or an animal to paint it properly," she says. "I used to tag along with my father when he was out doing survey work, and he spent hours teaching me about wildlife. You have to study the animals to get a real feel for them."

Sally has been an avid angler and hunter her entire life and frequently accompanies one of her sons who breeds prize coon hounds on forays into the forest at night to monitor the dogs' performance.

She and her former husband operated a charter fishing boat business on Tybee for a number of years, and Sally still joins her sons on deep sea fishing trips. "It's just marvelous out there on the water," she smiles. "You never know what you're going to get or what you're going to see. Sometimes you don't get much of anything, but it's still wonderful to be out there."

In spite of her talent and popularity, Sally says painting does not top her priority list, lagging far behind skeet shooting, hunting, fishing, and horses.

Horses have attracted her since she was a child in Savannah, where she rode at stables just off DeRenne Avenue when it was still a dirt road.

Sally was a talented jumper for a number of years, participating frequently in equestrian shows, and it

Sally inspects one of her recent paintings.

was horses that she initially painted when she took up art as a child. "That's all I would paint back then," she says. "I just loved horses."

Her affinity for horses still clearly lingers. Sally treated herself to a special birthday present recently when she purchased a show-quality mare. "She's a jumper," says Sally. "She's registered under one of those high-falutin names, but we just call her Sally."

The four-legged Sally is currently "on her honeymoon" and is expected to foal any day now, according to the artist, who stables her mare in the company of other horses on her daughter's farm in South Carolina.

"All of my children love the outdoors," she says. "They may never be rich or famous, but they are all wonderful and they have wonderful lives."

When they were in their late teens, her sons were treated to a two-year, around-the-world excursion on a large sailing yacht, the owners of which invited them along as a special tribute to Sally, who had done a painting for them.

"They sailed to hundreds of places around the world," she smiles. "It was the experience of a lifetime. They finally flew back home when one of my boys got homesick for his Mamma while they were in Tahiti."

Sally says she was delighted that her boys had the unusual sailing experience, but she missed them terribly while they were gone and was delighted when they announced their return from the Pacific Island.

Her first paintings were watercolors; then she tried oils, but her favorite medium, acrylics, was discovered by happenstance. "I purchased some paint back in the late 1950s, and I didn't even look at what I was buying," she explains. "When I got home and took it out it was like pudding! I couldn't believe it.

"Then I started working with it and I was wild about it. Acrylics dry so rapidly they are great for me. I hate sitting around waiting for something to dry like you do with oils. Acrylic is just wonderful. I wouldn't work with anything else!"

While Sally's exquisite sea scenes have brought her fame, and it is these that most of her clients covet and encourage her to produce, she says they are not her favorite art form these days.

"I've been doing them for so long I'm getting tired of them, and in the early days I was painting frantically from 8 a.m. until 5 p.m. every day, just grinding them out. The gallery owners were getting rich, and I was doing OK, but it was just too much!"

She is currently gaining substantial satisfaction from her work on a sequence of paintings of forests and animals bearing little resemblance to her familiar scenes of sand dunes and seas.

"Not everybody's going to like these, but I like them, and this is what I want to do," she says, fingering through several stacks on the floor of her studio display room.

Acrylic paints and brushes await Sally in her studio.

Most of those recent paintings feature a soft shroud of early morning mist creating a mystic aura that makes one want to step into the painting to savor the peace it portrays.

Sally has been approached recently to put on a single-artist show featuring her new work "but it's too early to say for sure," she says. "I'll have to produce a lot more for a show, maybe as many as 70 paintings, and I have trouble keeping up with all the orders for my other work as it is."

If you drive slowly down South Campbell and look closely, you may see Sally most days working at the kitchen table in her house, which she calls the Hermit Crab Studios.

You'll also get an early introduction to her when you first arrive on the island. It was Sally who designed that colorful sign beside Highway 80, just after you cross the Lazaretto Creek bridge. It features the words "Tybee Island" against a background of her familiar depiction of sea, sand, and soaring seagulls.

Sally says she expects to remain on the island pretty much forever, "although I'm not one of those who rave about how great everything is and how terrific all the people are.

"I know it has a dark side. But I do love the nature of the place and the wildlife...and that view over the marsh is wonderful."

POSTSCRIPT: Sally Bostwick passed away on April 11, 2008, shortly after she moved to Bullock County to be with her children.

Albert Seidl -
Swashbuckling Sailor Drops His Anchor Here

An Adventurous Renaissance Man Turns to Art

Some folks defy categorization.

Their accomplishments and interests are far too varied for those convenient little adjectives we use to describe people as being "a this" or "a that."

Albert Seidl is one of these.

Albert Seidl paints shrimp boats on Lazeretto Creek.

This chunky, white-bearded Santa Claus look-alike is a quintessential Renaissance man who is equally adept as a designer and builder of boats and furniture; a gifted artist who is comfortable in painting, writing, sculpting (in wood, clay, bronze, and steel) and scrimshaw; and a cabinetmaker who creates fine moldings and other home accoutrements from wood.

But most of all, perhaps - despite his jolly old elf appearance - Albert is a swashbuckling sailor who has plied the seas aboard a boat built with his own hands in pursuit of adventures most of us only dream about.

He has ridden tidal waves, retrieved sunken treasure from a shipwreck in a remote area of the Pacific Ocean, and delved into the mysteries of the Bermuda Triangle.

This intrepid seafaring man tied not only his ship, but his heart and fortunes to Savannah when he sailed the barkentine Barba Negra - the picturesque tall ship that has become a fixture in its berth beside River Street - here from Europe almost a quarter of a century ago.

But such sea lovers can't remain hove to forever, and this sailing artist hoists his anchor with some frequency. One of his most recent voyages was aboard a wooden square-rigger dodging icebergs in the Arctic.

Albert, who received formal training at Folkwang Academy of Fine Arts in Essen, Germany, may be best known nowadays as a renowned artist whose paintings and sculptures have been featured at one-man shows in

22 countries.

Equally at ease painting in oil, gouache, watercolor, or acrylics, he says he enjoys strolling through downtown Savannah with his easel. He finds special inspiration "when the light is in just the right mood and I see something in a different light that I think I haven't seen before I sit down and start painting immediately. Sometimes I'm finished in two or three hours."

His most recent exhibition was held at Savannah's Lobby Gallery in November, and he's now heading to the Bahamas over the Christmas holidays for another.

Many of his paintings reaffirm his adoration of the sea through nautical motifs, as does his work with scrimshaw, the age-old sailor's art of carving the teeth, tusks, and bones of sea creatures.

And Albert has a yen to live yet closer to the water. He's looking to lease or purchase a lighthouse as his choice of abode.

Lighthouses rank among his favorite subjects to paint as well. He has adorned several canvasses with images of the Tybee Lighthouse and is planning another sequence soon.

His second residence of choice for communing with his creative muse is a windmill.

A heroic spirit permeates the Seidl family tree.

Albert painting the Tybee Lighthouse.

Both of Albert's sons are sea captains.

His grandfather was one of Germany's first flyers, leading a German air wing based in Russia during World War I.

Albert's father hitchhiked his way through the war zone to join his dad and became the wing's "mascot," later flying with pilots on combat missions during which he dropped grenades as they passed over target zones.

At 15, Albert's dad became the youngest German combat pilot ever.-.and perhaps the youngest one in the world. He flew with Germany's famous "Red Baron" and got to know American ace Eddie Rickenbacker when the latter was shot down over Germany. After a brief internment, Rickenbacker was returned to Allied forces during what was then a standard "gentleman's agreement" exchange of captured pilots.

Albert's dad renewed his acquaintance with Rickenbacker after the war when the two, joined by a French flyer they met during the war, started a company called Sky Writing Unlimited that sprinkled the skies with ad slogans created with puffs of smoke from their planes.

Rickenbacker later went on to head General Motors. Years later, Albert helped make repairs on Rickenbacker's yacht when the damaged vessel was tied up at St. Thomas in the U.S. Virgin Islands.

Born in the industrial Ruhr Valley city of Essen in 1935, Albert remained in Germany throughout World War II while his father was in charge of camouflage for Germany's air force.

Albert joined the militaristic Hitler Youth at encampments in his early teens, learning to shoot a rifle and a bazooka as he joined other young and elderly German men who were preparing to become the country's last line of defense when the bulk of Germany's fighting forces were depleted.

Happily, Germany surrendered before he was called to serve in this capacity.

Albert remembers the horrors of the war; each day at dusk the family climbed down into the bunker his father built in their yard to protect themselves from the nightly Allied bombings of his town.

"Our house was mostly demolished in the bombing," says Albert, who recalls emerging from the shelter after one such raid to find the entire city in flames, bodies littering the streets and crews from downed planes dangling from trees in the shrouds of their parachutes.

"I still have bad memories of that scene," he says.

Following the war, Albert - who had sketched and built boat models since he was a child - received his art degree from Folkwang Academy of Fine Arts at age 20. He immediately started selling paintings and sculpture, while working as a typographer.

He still considers some of his best work to be a sequence of paintings depicting German coal miners laboring in poorly ventilated, incredibly hot tunnels far below the earth's surface. Conditions were so miserable that many miners wore nothing but shoes and helmets.

Those paintings, which at the time infuriated both mine owners and union officials, are now on permanent display in a museum in his hometown.

While he has loved the sea since childhood, having read voraciously about sailing ships, it was not until he visited Hamburg when he was 16 that he first saw the ocean.

"I stood on the beach and looked out at sea and - like everybody else - I wondered what was beyond the horizon," he says. "It was really so typical. That's really what makes you sail and travel because in your imagination everything on the other side is always greener."

Albert fed his love of the water by kayaking off the coast of Italy and in his early 20s, unlike most such sea gazers, transformed his dreams into reality by crossing that horizon when he emigrated to Canada. He settled in Vancouver, B.C., which he describes "as one of the finest places on earth."

Arriving with very little money, Albert made ends meet by working as a lumberjack in the Yukon. He continued painting and even found the time to teach imprisoned Indians art and craft techniques to enable them to find gainful employment when they were released.

When snow came early one winter, closing the timber camp, he returned to Vancouver where, as a chill descended over the city, he serendipitously stumbled into an auction house.

"They were serving hot coffee and donuts to those inside. I went in for the free food, but mostly to warm up," he said.

That was one of the most fortuitous moves Albert ever made. While warming his hands, he got into the spirit of the auction, making a winning bid of $7.50 for an old chest fastened with a large lock, the key to which was missing.

Albert wanted to open the trunk right there, but the auctioneer told him he had to get it out and open it elsewhere. "I was dressed like a lumberjack, and he was anxious to get rid of me," laughs Albert.

Once back at his lodgings, Albert had a locksmith make a key. He anxiously opened the trunk and quickly inspected its contents. Among them he discovered a painting that to his trained eye was very much in the style of noted artist William Turner. There was also a drawing that appeared to be the work of Flemish painter Franz Hals.

To verify his opinion, he took the paintings to an art gallery, but was told it would be necessary to send them to England to determine their authenticity.

Unable to pay the estimated $600 the gallery said such authentication would cost and uncertain whether the art was that of the famous painters or someone imitating their style, Albert accepted the gallery's offer of $3,000 on the spot, satisfied that he had struck it rich with his $7.50 investment.

A year later the gallery owner invited him to dinner where he congratulated him on his find, saying the paintings were the genuine articles. That was the good news, he said. The bad news was that he would get no more money.

The painting at the time was valued at about $30,000; the drawing about $20,000. On today's market they would likely be worth well over a million dollars, Albert said.

But art was not the only treasure in the trunk. There was also a logbook compiled by a sea captain named McDonald, who at the turn of the 20th century operated a sailing vessel hauling cargo from Canada to Australia and back.

The captain left no heirs when he died; the trunk purchased by Albert was part of his estate, items from which were sold by the government for back taxes at the auction.

The logbook, which Albert read from cover to cover, contained notations about McDonald's search for a treasure ship that had sunk near Cocos Island, 350 miles off the coast of Panama.

While on the island with two crewmen, McDonald's

ship dragged anchor and sank in a severe storm. Once the storm had passed, McDonald sailed a 24-foot gig almost 400 miles to Costa Rica, where he arrived alone.

Authorities held him there for questioning about the disappearance of his ship and crew but, with no one to contradict his story, McDonald was released and headed back to Canada where he says he became a partner in the Princess Line cruise ship company.

Reading the logbook sparked Albert's spirit of adventure, luring him irrevocably to the sea. To get there he undertook the Herculean task of building a 58-foot wooden ketch in the yard of his Vancouver home.

"All of my knowledge about building boats came out of a little library where I used to go religiously every night to read everything I could find," says Albert.

He obtained the drawings for his vessel from noted naval architect William Garden after becoming enamored of his design in a yachting magazine. Albert traveled to Seattle, Wash. to meet with Garden and purchase his drawings.

Albert discusses his art.

He was chagrined to learn they were priced at $10,000 but was delighted when the designer agreed to trade them for two of his paintings. "I had a trunk full of paintings and told him he could have them all in exchange for the drawings. But he said fair is fair, your work for mine, and took two paintings for two drawings," smiles the artist, who admits at the time he was getting only about $500 for his paintings.

Albert acquired much of the estimated $30,000 in material for his boat by bartering his art (the sails were made in England in trade for a single painting), and he became a celebrity in Vancouver during his four-year construction project when newspapers and magazines published intermittent articles about his progress.

That publicity proved valuable because it prompted seamen to stop by to inspect his craft when they passed through the area. Many of those mariners invited Albert out for cruises aboard their boats.

Albert, who had never taken a ship to sea, paid careful attention to the sailors, talking with them for hours about sailing techniques. One English seaman even gave him instructions in celestial navigation. "I must admit that he had immense patience," laughs Albert. "I was not a quick learn."

His growing notoriety also proved handy when the boat was completed and moving it from his yard to the harbor some 18 miles away posed a problem.

Albert's solution was to work out a deal with operators

of a shopping center in the city. They displayed his boat in their parking lot for a month to draw customers in payment for which they hauled it to the water.

During that month Pierre Trudeau, who was running for the post of prime minister of Canada, used Albert's boat as a platform for a stirring speech about taking the country's helm and guiding it into a brighter future.

Immediately after launching his craft, christened Illhaee, an Indian name meaning "all my belongings," Albert set sail on a dual adventure.

In conjunction with famous writer and seaman Thor Hyerdahl, he participated in an expedition to trace the route Canadian Indians followed to Pacific islands, heading south from Canada in huge canoes, then turning west to Easter Island and the South Sea islands beyond, where fragments of their language and designs still exist.

In a tribute to the publicity they received in conjunction with the expedition and Albert's earlier work teaching tribal members arts and crafts, an Indian tribe native to Vancouver Island made him an honorary chief.

"I'd always dreamed about things like that as a child, but you never imagine it could happen," smiles Albert. "It was quite an honor."

The Hyerdahl expedition was only part of Albert's plan. He was determined to sail to Cocos Island in search of McDonald's sunken vessel.

But one night while cruising along the coast of Mexico, he got more than most seamen bargain for. "The ocean rose beneath the boat, and I was carried along for miles," he says.

It was only when Albert spotted the lights of San Carlos on the Bay of Magdalena behind him - when they had just been far ahead, albeit his compass setting had not changed - that he realized the incredible speed at which his boat was moving.

Albert was sitting atop the tail end of a mountainous tidal wave spawned in Alaska which ultimately deposited his craft 500 yards inland on a barren stretch of the Mexican coast.

The wave simply rose under him and carried his boat about 80 miles in a single hour "with no warning, and I didn't even feel it," he says.

When the wave reached the Continental Shelf where the water became shallower, it started to break with tremendous turbulence. The moment he heard that deafening sound, "I knew I was in deep trouble," Albert says. "We landed in the second row of dunes in the desert."

Though miraculously uninjured, he was now in a

Looking over Albert Seidl's shoulder while he paints on Tybee.

quandary as to how to get his boat back to water. After pondering the problem for several days, he became both relieved and concerned when a Mexican Navy ship approached the site.

His worries evaporated when a team of sailors from the ship immediately initiated efforts to free his boat. Unfortunately, during one of several futile attempts to drag the vessel to sea as the water receded a cable snapped, killing one of the Mexican sailors. Ultimately, they dug a channel to the stranded boat and floated it to deep water.

But before he could continue his voyage, a month of extensive repairs was required. As he was towed into a nearby port by the Mexicans, Albert worried about hair-raising rumors of robbers and "bandidos."

He was delighted to find that the Mexicans "were perfect gentlemen and took care of everything," including removing the boat's sand-engulfed engine, which they cleaned and replaced.

When their work was completed, the Mexicans filled his fuel tanks, and the admiral in charge of the facility invited Albert to his flagship for a banquet. While dining, Albert was plagued with nagging concerns about the cost of the rescue and repairs.

But when he called the admiral aside to ask what he owed for the work, the admiral turned around and told Albert, "Gringo, there are gentlemen in Mexico, and we have a few, so please enjoy your food." And, Albert added, "not a dime did they charge!"

Albert says he now has many friends in Mexico "because my attitude toward them was completely changed. I saw the other side of Mexico."

Once underway again, the Illhaee set sail for Cocos Island. Sailing single handed, following McDonald's log book, Albert located the land mass and spotted his sunken ship dangling precariously on the edge of a precipice beneath 80 feet of crystal clear water.

Descending to the wreck, Albert swam inside and scooped up a handful of emeralds as the vessel teetered on the edge, threatening to tumble into an abyss while a large school of sharks complicated the situation when they converged on the site.

"I was scared," says Albert, who quickly apprised the situation and scrambled swiftly to the surface. His panic-driven flight proved far too fast when he failed to decompress at stages during his rise. Blood was pouring from his ears when he climbed aboard his boat. Unable to hear a thing, he sailed to Panama in silence.

He was hospitalized in that country while undergoing several sessions of surgery that finally restored his hearing.

Later, Albert cruised to the Caribbean conducting charter excursions for three years, before sailing to San Diego where he sold the Illhaee for $140,000, then returned to Canada, where he hunkered down for a while painting and working on boat designs.

The designs became more than a hobby when an acquaintance, the admiral in charge of U.S. Navy operations in the Mekong Delta during the latter stages of the Vietnam War, inspected them. The admiral was fascinated by his design for a fast moving, 26-foot motor craft and hired Albert to supervise construction of a prototype for the vessels he utilized in that operation.

After 13 years residence in Canada, Albert was again overtaken by wanderlust and headed for Europe in search of a boat he could afford, unwilling, at that stage, to invest the time and energy necessary to build another himself.

Albert located one in Denmark, but the price was astronomical. So he headed for another town on the coast of Norway where he was told a 19th century barkentine was about to be destroyed.

At first glance he fell in love with the tall three-masted ship - which had been utilized for years as a cargo vessel but had become a derelict condemned by the government and bought it for $40,000.

Then he contacted Gerhard Schwisow, an old sailing buddy from his Caribbean cruising days, who wholeheartedly helped in the boat's restoration with a view toward joining Albert on future sailing adventures. The project, financed by Albert at considerable cost and personal labor, took three years, after which the now pristine barkentine was renamed Barba Negra, Spanish for Black Beard.

Before sailing to Savannah, however, the partners plied Scandinavian waters on scenic cruises and leased their colorful boat for use in pirate movies, after which they conducted cruises for tourists in the Caribbean.

Albert also became involved in a somewhat secret, often eerie study in the mystery shrouded Bermuda Triangle. The government-funded study involved testing underwater sound transmissions with exotic devices that could detect explosions as far away as Australia.

The tests enabled the government to determine the specific moment underwater explosions occurred, based on the time it took for the sound to reach the listening device.

"Sonic booms" resulting from the collision of different water temperatures were recorded as well. "It was those," Albert says scientists told him, "that could destroy anything in their wake" with the vibrations they generate. He says this may be the cause of many lost ships that simply "fell apart" in the Bermuda Triangle.

The prototype equipment could also determine directions underwater, permitting navigation by sound alone. But there were other intriguing sounds recorded on the instruments, which operated round the clock and could amplify volumes up to 200,000 times.

Albert says he heard shipboard activities and voices in dozens of different languages taking place on ships that could not be seen. He also heard thousands of shrimp flipping in the distance and whales communicating with noises so loud they would "blow you out of the room" unless the volume on the devices was quickly lowered.

"It was like a sound from outer space!" he recalls. "You could hear all sorts of things scattering when whales entered the area. Every living creature has its own peculiar sound."

Other more mysterious events occurred in the Triangle, but they "are taboo to talk about," says Albert ominously. Navy ships were dispatched frequently to fetch tapes of all the noises. Many were retained by the government, while others were returned with sections deleted.

Albert speculates that many Bermuda Triangle mysteries stem from "the density of the various water streams, the unusually deep water and its extreme variation in temperatures at relatively small changes in depth. "Something is happening there," he says, noting "when you're ignorant about certain things, they can mean a lot to you, but as you learn, they can become very simple and natural."

One example he cited was the impression one gets when a ship passes and seems to have "six or seven welders aboard because you see all the lights flashing, but it's a question of being in the right conditions for static fires."

Albert paints group attending Miller Avenue party on Tybee.

"All of a sudden the mast is on fire; the rail is on fire, and the whole ship is on fire, with flames coming out of everywhere. That's called St. Elmo's Light, and it's a 'cold' fire. You could touch it and it wouldn't burn."

Albert said he has seen this phenomenon in

the Pacific as well as the Bermuda Triangle, and it has occurred on his own vessel.

Ultimately, Albert and Gerhard sailed the Barba Negra to Savannah in the late 1970s to refurbish her at a shipyard in preparation for an extended tour of the South Pacific.

Based on his shipbuilding expertise and the work they witnessed on the Barba Negra, Navy officials hired Albert to restore a number of wooden World War II mine sweepers that had been stored in Charleston since the Korean War. Albert performed this work at a shipyard just east of Savannah in Thunderbolt, then lingered there for ten years refurbishing tugboats and yachts. He has remained in Savannah ever since.

The once proud Barba Negra remains berthed by River Street where she was tied up 20 years ago, never setting sail for the South Pacific.

Albert says he is saddened by her current state of disrepair. At one time he tried to establish a boat building school that would have refurbished the old barkentine as its first project before turning it over to a non-profit organization for use as a training vessel or to raise funds for charity and boost city tourism.

When he is not painting or holding exhibitions, Albert now spends most of his time writing a book about his sailing adventures and remodeling the rambling house he purchased in the city a decade ago.

He also helps out occasionally at Ice Cream, Etc., a shop operated adjacent Savannah's City Market by his wife, Alise, whom he met in Norway and wed aboard the Barba Negra in Long Island Sound.

But his heart is never far from the sea. Albert frequently visits and sails in Norway with his two sons, Mark and David, both of whom are captains of tall ships used for sail training. Mark, in true Seidl fashion, at age 34 became the youngest sail-training captain ever accredited in Norway.

Albert joined his sons a couple of years ago on a six-week voyage aboard a huge square rigger through the iceberg-strewn waters of the Arctic, replicating the voyage of early seafarers on the first Polar expedition. "That was a dream come true, a real adventure, and I'm really proud of my boys," he says.

Albert is now building a small sailing dinghy and says he's contemplating construction of a larger vessel similar to the one he created for his first excursion from Canada. "I may just build another one," he smiles, a wistful look crossing his face as he considers the possibility and recalls his adventures at sea.

At that moment it seems he would be more comfortable at a ship's wheel than a painter's palette and - if his now booming art sales don't anchor him down - you can bet he will.

POSTSCRIPT: Albert Seidl was a prominent member of the Brotherhood of the Coast, an international fraternity of seafarers for which he hosted a gathering on Tybee Island. Albert, who passed away on May 3, 2019, became an acclaimed artist and established a studio in Savannah's Market Square. His widow, Alise Seidl, held a memorial service for Albert on the shore of the Back River on Tybee during which his ashes were placed aboard a model Viking ship which was set afire as it sailed into the sunset.

Burning model of Viking ship sets sail during memorial service.

Sinbad - Hard-Living Old Sailor Rules Island Street

Former Bar Owner Named Street's "Mayor"

He's Sinbad, the mayor of 16th Street, perhaps forever.

That's where he hangs out now, over at the arcade and the bars along the 16th street strip.

'Course it's called Tybrisa now. But Tybee's old timers have trouble breaking ingrained habits. Besides, since Sinbad is the elected "Mayor of 16th Street," it'll always be that to him.

You just know from looking at the guy that he had to have been a sailor… and he was, for a number of years. Sinbad has tattoos up and down his arms, a flowing beard and long hair, both grown white from 67 years of right hard living.

The tattoos work with his other love beyond the sea as well. He was a biker for years. Harleys of course. But he had a couple of Indians as well, way back when. He wishes he still had those babies. They'd be worth a fortune now.

Sinbad traded his last Hog, along with an El Camino, about ten years ago for a houseboat on the Back River. "Boat sank, but you live and learn," Sinbad smiles.

Nothing much seems to rile the old boy. He kind of lets life flow like the tides. That word "old" might do it though. Sinbad, whose last wife was 25 years younger than him, still hankers after the girls and figures he probably will forever, literally.

"I told my son, whenever I go, I want you to cremate me and pour half my ashes down 16th Street where I can watch my drunks and my partners and the other half on the beach in front of 16th street where I can watch the bikinis come by."

Sinbad dropped anchor on the island, or near it, at Ft. Pulaski to be precise, about 23 years ago. He was a tugboat captain at the time. Boat's name was Captain Roy.

Sinbad was hauling material to a spot just across from the fort where a docking facility for large container ships was to be built by Diamond Construction Co. Ships were to unload their cargo at that spot, where it would be picked up by smaller boats and hauled upriver.

Sinbad hugs his daughter, Lynell, just after she married Troy Burdette during surf-side ceremonies on Tybee's beach.

One of the two ships initially scheduled to use it, a Dutch vessel, sank with all hands aboard enroute from Europe. Sinbad doesn't rightly know what happened to the other one. But the docking facility was never completed. You can still see the old steel beams he hauled if you look toward the far shore from the fort. "Just a pile of metal over there now," says Sinbad. "Probably nobody knows what it was for."

After that, Sinbad dropped anchor on Tybee where he's been hanging out ever since. "Haven't been off the island for more than a month since I got here," he says.

Hanging out is exactly what he mostly does now although, when he first arrived, he owned and operated two bars at the south end. The first was - where else? - on 16th Street, at the site of the present Windrose Cafe.

Sinbad says lousy management closed that bar, and he got another one, around the corner, where the Blind Pelican bar and restaurant is now located.

"We did a great business there," he says. "Place was always crowded." It was the island's politics that drove him out of that one, he says.

"I figure somebody just had it in for me. Nobody bothered the previous owners for 20 years, but, when I took over, the health and building inspectors were always on my back. They made me put in a new ceiling and new floors and new sinks. Cost me a bunch."

Sinbad says he sort of lost the urge for entrepreneurship after that and started working at the bars along 16th Street and around the corner on Butler Ave. "I've worked at every one of 'em."

But he never goes to the north end, except to drive through on brief trips off the island or go to the post office. "You turn 20-mile curve (at Tybee's north end, now called Kuhlman's Corner), that's Yankee land up there. It's the difference between north and south."

And, looking down the street from his apartment's porch, also - you guessed it - on 16th Street, he notes: "Got everything I need right here. Don't have to drive anywhere. I can walk to whatever I need." He is, however, a bit distressed that they moved the old post office, formerly located directly across the street from his place, to north end "Yankee land."

Sinbad takes a stand on 16th Street.

Though he's embedded a full root system in Tybee's sand over the years, Sinbad's originally from Riverside, California. He joined the Navy on his 17th birthday and made a career of it - 20 years - retiring at the age of 37, while he was stationed in Norfolk, Virginia.

After his retirement, he returned to Riverside, operated a couple of bars there for a bit, and then purchased and operated a seagoing salvage tugboat there for a while.

That ended abruptly, however, when he returned to Norfolk for a visit with his kids (he had six of 'em by a wife he was married to for 16 years while in the service). Sinbad got a frantic call from the West Coast during that visit strongly suggesting that he not return home.

Seems somebody had borrowed his tug while he was away and made a trip down to Mexico. When it got back, it had five tons of a questionable plant aboard which was confiscated, along with the boat, his Mercedes, and his turbocharged Corvair Monza. That was 30 years ago, and Sinbad has not sailed that coast since.

It was in Norfolk that he picked up the name Sinbad. (Don't tell anyone but his given name is Donnie Dinwiddie.)

"It was during an argument with my girlfriend," he said. "We were both pretty drunk, and she started yelling at me and said 'you just live a life of fantasy, you and your damned boat. They oughta call you Sinbad'. And the name stuck. Nobody's called me anything else since."

Sinbad got himself a 50-foot motorboat on which he lived, and a tugboat while in Norfolk and made runs up and down the east coast on the tug. Then he moved to Savannah, where he also operated that tug near Ft. Pulaski for a while before finally turning landlubber on Tybee.

It was a woman who ran the old sailor aground. "My wife was with her family, and I was living on the tug, and I drove over to Tybee to get some provisions. I went into the old Anchor Inn on 16th Street, and met this girl and just fell in love," he says.

She was 25 years his junior. Sinbad got unhitched and re-hitched. His third wife, like his second, died at an early age not long ago.

The "Mayor of 16th Street" title was earned, somewhat legitimately, in a real election participated in by bar owners and customers along the strip. Sinbad got the vast majority, 211 votes, in the election, which was held back in 1991.

His election was the lead story in the 16th Street Gazette, a bawdy and short-lived newspaper published by Jim "Mayonnaise" Green, one of the island's more colorful characters.

"It's legal now, Sinbad is the undisputed mayor, the people have spoken," an island attorney was quoted as saying in the Gazette story.

"We just decided we needed our own government on the south end 'cause we were a different place, a separate entity," he said. "We elected our own council and everything." The mayor and council met sporadically when they bumped into one another in various bars.

Sinbad says his major activity as mayor "was drinking, supporting the local businessmen." But that's been awhile, and, according to Sinbad, he's cut down on his drinking and kind of settled down since then, relaxing on his porch, admiring the models of old Harley Davidson and Indian motorcycles he keeps in his place, and, of course, watching those bikinis.

He still puts in a day's work occasionally at the nearby arcade on 16th and Butler and he's got a steady girlfriend now who he met not long ago.

Sinbad's not only the mayor; he's the king of 16th Street, and, given his burial plans, he'll be there forever.

POSTSCRIPT: Sinbad may no longer be with us physically, but many old timers believe his spirit still lingers along 16th Street, perhaps grimacing over the fact that his beloved street's name has been changed to Tybrisa.

Linda Odom -
The Hat Lady Blazes a Wide Trail

Promoting Her Way to Success

She's called "The Hat Lady" and lives in (take your pick) "The Alligator" or "Tybrisa Two."

Linda Odom is an attractive bundle of energy as she flits around her beach house to grab the phone, a cup of coffee, or to fetch one of her haughty hats. She loves her hats and her house, and her affinity for the former led to her nickname.

"People couldn't remember my name, but they recalled my always wearing a hat, so that's what they began to call me: 'The Hat Lady'," she says.

"Jack Youmans (long-time Tybee city councilman) would just refer to me as 'that lady in the hat at the Chamber of Commerce,' and that's where it probably started. I just love to wear them."

But don't be misled by her feminine fascination for hats. She's a trailblazer for women in business, particularly those moving into formerly male-dominated professions.

Back in the '60s, she became one of the first female "salesmen" for Boyle Midway, handling Woolite sales and marketing throughout the southeast. "I was their first token woman," she recalls, remembering how she had to work longer, harder, and smarter to make it in this competitive field where most of the salesmen were old-line males.

"I wore pantsuits and vests and kept my hair cut short and brushed back to try to blend in," she says. "At that time it was difficult being a female."

Linda knew she was facing a pivotal moment when she sat down with the crusty old owner of a warehouse in Jacksonville who serviced most of the outlets in the southeast. He was her first major account.

"The first thing he asked me was if I was one of those bra-burning, liberated females," she recalls. "I said, no sir, I wouldn't consider myself one of those liberated females. I don't burn my bras. They're much too expensive. And if I was liberated, I'd be sittin' down at Ponte Vedra sippin' a cool one. I wouldn't be up here hustling the streets trying to sell you Woolite."

He laughed uproariously and became one of Linda's biggest customers. "He bought every product we carried," she smiles. And, while it didn't make her very popular with fellow salesmen, Linda became one of the company's most successful salespeople.

Although she grew up in Jesup, Linda feels she's a native of Tybee and Savannah. "We were always in Savannah and Tybee for the beach and for shopping and going to the doctor and dentist," she says. "It was the only place to go."

After attending Georgia Southern University in Statesboro, Linda decided that secretarial or accounting work was not her cup of tea. She wound up in Macon, in a training position with an employment agency.

"I figured if I wanted a really good job the best place to find one was as an employment counselor," she says. That opportunity came when she saw the opening with Boyle Midway.

It was about this time that Linda also experienced what she calls "a short marriage. It lasted only two years." But that wasn't her briefest marriage. After moving to Tybee in 1978 ("when it wasn't really fashionable to live here"), she was married again, for just three months, and that one hardly seemed to count.

"It was just sort of passing the time," she says. "I had dates that lasted longer than that marriage."

Linda says she purchased the large old house in which she still lives to establish a stable base. After a while, she grew tired of roaming the country with Woolite sales.

She recalls she was in Birmingham, when she got the urge to return to her roots and joined Dick Estes' Outdoor Advertising Co. in Savannah, becoming its first female sales representative.

She soon found herself on the road again, now selling billboard advertising, but found solace in having a firm base at the beach. "When I came home on weekends, I'd close the door on the car and never get back in until it was time for me to leave the following week," she says. "It was really nice."

It was also pretty lively at what became known as "Tybrisa Two." Linda was more or less camping out in her spacious old house while working on its renovation "and people kept kind of breezing in and breezing out," she says. "All my friends came down."

"I told everyone they were welcome to stay, even if I wasn't around." Many took her at her word, turning her house into a party pad.

Linda recalls a guy named Louie who was the tenant in a cottage behind her house. "We called him Hemingway" because he was a prolific writer and island wanderer, she says.

"Hemingway always had a trumpet with him and would play taps every night." He also played reveille early each morning, awakening not only Linda and her fellow revelers, but the entire neighborhood.

Ultimately, the trumpeting troubadour was drawn to the sea, purchased a sailboat and is now "sailing around the world somewhere," says Linda. "I'm sure he's having a wonderful time." The cottage where he lived is long gone. Her spacious swimming pool now occupies that space.

Linda is ready for a party.

Linda remembers her mother's remorse on learning of Hemingway's departure. "Who's going to play the trumpet for Monica (Linda's daughter and an infant at that time)?" her mother asked.

Linda allows as how her mother was unaware of the extent of the riotous times at her house. "When Mom came to visit, we kept things very proper," she laughs, except, of course, for Hemingway, who was not that easy to control.

She also recalls a young female tenant of a downstairs apartment she once rented, who ran screaming into the street one morning, clad only in a towel. "She woke the entire neighborhood," says Linda, "everyone stood staring at her."

A partying prankster had placed one of those then-popular thigh-high toy robots in the young lady's shower, and she freaked out when she spotted it.

If you want to hear about Linda's more colorful parties, you can forget about it. She's circumspect about such things now because of concern for her young daughter, to whom she is obviously devoted and more than a little protective.

Truth be told, life was not always a constant party in those days since Linda was dead serious about her work. She became east-coast manager for the national firm to which Estes sold his company; left that position to become a promotional representative for area hotels; then sold real estate for a while before becoming a registered tour guide for the Savannah Historic Society.

"But I wanted to do my own thing, and I felt tours should be expanded to the entire coast rather than Savannah alone," she says. That's when she sold a "Deep South Tour" package idea to a New Jersey firm specializing in long-distance bus tours.

The agreement called for ten busloads of tourists to be brought down each week for extended tours of Charleston, Beaufort, and Hilton Head in South Carolina in addition to Savannah. Linda was to provide tour guides for each location and arrange for hotel accommodations and meals.

But she had no tour guides or agenda and nothing except her Historic Savannah experience as far as knowledge for such an operation. She had six months to get ready to meet her obligation and the good fortune of having Savannah's promotional wizard, Jeanne Cahn, as a close friend.

Jeanne was the first director of Savannah's downtown River Street Association and one of the key people developing the city's fledging tourist industry in the late '60s and '70s. When Linda called on her, Jeanne quickly put together a script to be used for each of the tour cities and helped Linda train tour guides. When they ran short of guides, Jeanne even took over one of the tour buses to help her friend.

"I couldn't have done it without her," says Linda, who claims Jeanne, along with Dick Estes, were instrumental in making Savannah the tourist mecca it is today. "They ought to erect a monument in Savannah to Jeanne and Dick."

"They did more than anyone to promote tourism in the city, and they've never gotten proper credit. It was Jeanne who started the riverfront festivals and the street vendors. She started Oktoberfest, and now it's so crowded you can't even get down there."

Ultimately, Linda's tour was a great success, leading to an ongoing relationship with the New Jersey firm and the formation of her own company, "Tales of the South Tour Guides," which she still operates.

She has established an office in Savannah and expanded her tour services to St. Simons and Jekyll Islands and the Okefenokee Swamp.

On Tybee, Linda serves on the board of directors of the Chamber of Commerce and St. Michaels Catholic School. She's also been active - and tried to be more so - in developing Tybee tourism.

Back in 1992, she was asked to take over the Beach Music Festival which had been initiated the previous year with a relatively shaky start. Linda accepted the assignment only after her friend Jeanne agreed to help her.

The festival, held in the former open area between the DeSoto Beach Hotel and the former Econo Lodge, featured name bands and vendors selling food and merchandise. By the second year, under her direction, it was drawing thousands, and plans were well underway to stage the biggest festival ever the following year.

Linda says continued use of the property became an issue; the city refused to allow the beach to be used as a festival site, and the lack of commitment for a location, combined with substantial upfront payment requirements for entertainers, led to the festival's demise.

"I still get phone calls from people in Atlanta who remember it and want to come again," says Linda, who feels the city missed a real opportunity to draw in tourist dollars.

She also attempted to stage a street dance along 16th

Street (now Tybrisa) in conjunction with and following the annual beachfront fireworks display on July 3, but hit a roadblock when the city refused to ban parking on 16th for the street festivities.

Linda says she thought such a dance, with tables and chairs along the block, would draw additional crowds and ease the traffic snarl following the fireworks by encouraging people to linger for the party rather than departing in a traffic snarl after the fireworks.

"The crowd of dancers along the street might even wander into the adjacent shops and buy some things," helping local business, she said, noting that all that was needed was for the city to provide extra police for security and block off the street, since the Chamber of Commerce had already agreed to pay for the dance band.

Linda feels she failed to gain sufficient support for the plan because some folks felt the fireworks were already drawing more than enough people "but I still think it's a good idea and it ought to be done."

In her early days on Tybee, Linda also tried to get old-time ice cream trucks to cruise the island and stage parties for kids and older people, but she failed to win approval for that plan as well.

Undeterred, she is still an avid supporter of any activity which will draw tourists, "and I'd love to do more promotions on the island, but not right now. I got too emotionally involved, too close to it. I had to step back. My family now comes first."

Linda looking good in black.

She's enthusiastic about the future of Tybee's annual jazz festival which was held for the first time this year. "Anything that people do well on Tybee just tickles me to death," she says.

And she's optimistic about the new pavilion, which she believes is a great location for bands and other entertainment. She would like to see programs there every month to draw people out from Savannah.

Linda also thinks the island should offer more in the way of family activities and entertainment for tourists and for island residents.

"If you're single and like to drink, there's plenty to keep you busy, but there's very little for families with children to do," she laments.

One recent bright spot, she says, was this year's Halloween haunted house for island children, which had a large turnout. Tybee really needs a full-time special events person to develop activities and bring in more business, according to Linda, who says she wouldn't seek that position because "most people feel a promotion position is only a part-time thing and worth only part-time pay."

While she's not available for big-time island promotions now, you might consider contacting her in six years or so when things may be different.

Monica will be 17 then and "when they get their driver's license, that's when they're gone, absolutely gone," says Linda, wincing at the thought.

Until then, she wants to spend all the time she can with her daughter. "I just love her so much," she says. "She's my baby doll. I enjoy every minute I spend with her." That's the principal reason she's reduced her activities with Tales of the South, closing the Savannah office and moving the business to her home on Tybee.

But she says she's not entirely through with promotions, just those for which she gets paid. Linda's busy right now promoting the first of what she hopes will become annual golf tournaments and dances to raise funds for St. Michaels School, which has no lunch facilities.

Students now eat at their classroom desks, and Linda hopes to raise enough money to provide fold out tables for the school gymnasium and eventually enough to construct a facility for a real lunchroom.

The first golf tournament is to be held next April at the Sheraton golf course on Wilmington Island. Linda hopes to stage the dance "to be open to the entire island," on the new pavilion.

Meanwhile, her house has been transformed into a beach show place, with beveled glass doors and a "Tybee room" (she refuses to use the term "Florida room") furnished with bright, overstuffed sofas and chairs.

Handsome antiques adorn each of the many warm, wood-paneled rooms, and a formal, sunlit dining room appears ready for a dinner party with a linen tablecloth and napkins, place settings and sparkling crystal glasses all perfectly arranged.

But the tasteful accoutrements don't represent a total change for the house. It's still a party place. The difference is that now the gatherings are mostly for Monica and her classmates.

"Our pool has become the community swimming pool for the St. Michael's kids, and I love it," says Linda, who keeps tabs on the activities below while sitting on the expansive deck off the second floor of her house overlooking the pool.

Even though her house appears to be picture perfect, Linda says it's still a work in progress which likely will never be completed, and that's what led to the pad's recent reincarnation as "The Alligator."

Carroll, her husband in what she calls "my only real marriage," hung that label on the place shortly after he moved in and learned that work on the house swallowed most of their time and money like a ravenous alligator.

They've been married 12 years now but have known one another since they attended high school together in Jesup. He was the best dancer in school, did the best shag in the entire area," says Linda, who apparently wasn't too shabby at cutting a rug herself in those days.

They maintained contact, through his marriage and two of hers, but the relationship was never romantic until they started dating years later. "Something just happened after all those years," says Linda.

Meanwhile, Carroll and Monica are fortunate that Linda appears to have her omnipresent hat on straight as she dashes about "Tybrisa Two," aka "The Alligator," creating a special life for them at the beach.

The rest of us will just have to wait another half dozen years to see if Linda leaps back into the fray of the island's promotions and politics.

POSTSCRIPT: Linda Odom remains on Tybee and continues to operate her successful travel business. Her marriage has remained intact, while her daughter, Monica, now grown, has flown the

nest, moving to Washington, D.C. where she is now happily married and has three children of her own.

Michael Hosti -
Grocer Has Long History on Tybee

Service to Island Runs In the Family

Mike Hosti

Michael Hosti, one of that extended family on Tybee which numbered 163 at last count, including uncles, aunts, and cousins, may be the clan's best known current member.

Newcomers may not realize there's such a host of Hostis "because we mostly had girls, and their names changed when they married," according to Michael, who's one of the few family members without a nickname or hands-on political experience.

Michael's uncle Charley was a three-term Tybee mayor, but no one called him Charley. He went by the name George. And there's usually a Hosti on city council. One, a nephew who is also named Michael, is a current councilman known as Spec.

His nephew Spec's family exemplifies the female trait in the Hosti line. He's the only male among eight siblings. One of his seven sisters also served on council, as did his uncle Michael's uncle Ernest.

Then there was Michael's father, Benno. He was called Mike and served on city council for 25 years. Michael himself was named for his father's nickname.

Aunt Sal incidentally was called Sophie.

Michael is the purveyor of the island's most necessary non-alcoholic commodity... food. He owns and operates Tybee's IGA Market, the only supermarket east of Wilmington Island.

Beefy and well over six-feet tall, Michael is an imposing figure. Save for his professorial-looking grey mustache and goatee, he looks more like a barroom brawler than a grocery store proprietor.

Scratch the surface, however, and you'll find an incredibly hardworking man with a tenderloin nature and a heart as soft as melted butter.

And that facial hair is not necessarily misleading. He's a history buff who graduated magna cum laude from Draughon's College, which he attended at night while working full time as manager of the market.

Michael has spent his entire life on the island and has been active at his grocery store since the age of six when he started sweeping up, bagging groceries, and doing odd jobs in order to spend more time with his father, who began operating a store on the same site beginning in the 1930s.

"It wasn't that he didn't want to spend time with me at home," says Michael. "It was just that the grocery business is the most time-consuming business there is. There wasn't time for anything else.

"By the time I was 12, I was working there every day after school and for 14 to 16 hours on Saturdays and Sundays. I grew to love the grocery business as much as my father did."

Michael cherished their relationship and still gets a trifle misty-eyed when he recalls those days. "Over the years he was the best partner I ever had," he says. "I can't think of a better friend or business associate than my Dad. We never had a fight in all those years.

"I listened to everything he said…didn't always follow his advice, although he was right most of the time, but I listened and remembered."

There was one piece of advice he did follow and still does.

"I was running around with a pretty wild group of friends at one time, and most of the time you get into wild things it's because of peer pressure," he says.

"Dad called me in for a talk and said some days he really worried about me. I asked what he meant, and he said it was the friends I was running with."

"He said he felt bad about saying anything about it and that he didn't want me to think he wanted to pick my friends for me because your friends are your friends, and I don't understand them like you do, but I want you to remember something for the rest of your life. Just remember that the people you feel are your friends may not always be your friends and beware of what they're gonna get you into."

"You might be called a chicken or yellow bellied or whatever, but just remember it takes a lot bigger man to walk away from it than it does to get into it."

Mike looks over his grocery store.

"On many occasions when I could have gotten into serious trouble that thought came back to me. I've always lived by that theory and do 'til this day. I'm very leery of people that I feel are just a little bit too much on the wild side."

Despite such caution, no one ever called Michael a "Goody Two Shoes" since he sowed his share of wild oats as a kid. “Smoked a little pot, did some drugs and stuff, but that’s all history now,” he says. “I did some stuff that I’m not real proud of, but at the same time those things were all a lesson.”

“It just keeps me from going back and doing the same thing again. It’s a learning experience. Every day’s a learning experience. If I don’t learn something new every day, I feel like I’ve wasted a day.”

As to barroom brawls, he’s had his share of fights but says he walks away from them when he can, regardless of the risk of ridicule. “Somebody my size, everybody wants a piece of to show how tough they are,” he says. “I’ve had my butt whipped a few times in my lifetime, and I’ve whipped a few butts in my lifetime, but basically, I’m a nonviolent person. I don’t want to be a bad ass. Unless I’m really backed into a corner I’ll walk away. It’s really not worth the trouble.”

Michael continued working in the store through grade school at St. Michael’s on the island and high school at Johnson in Savannah.

When his father was ill for a couple of months while he was attending high school, Michael ran the store for him, keeping up with his classes by driving into Savannah to pick up and drop off assignments and going in for tests.

That didn’t seem detrimental to his scholarship. Michael skipped the eleventh grade at Johnson and led his class at Draughon's College, where he majored in accounting and business administration.

"I learned to get an education at St. Michael's," he says, chuckling at the recollection. "They had all nuns there when I attended, and if you didn't learn, they took a stick and beat it in you. They cracked my knuckles a number of times."

Once out of high school, he became the fulltime manager of the Tybee Market and has remained intimately involved with its operation ever since. It's not just a job to Michael. It's pretty much his entire life, save for occasional excursions to local bistros to unwind.

He has a reputation as one of Tybee's best dancers and is a popular partner for a number of island ladies.

One of the regulars at Doc's Bar, Michael maneuvers his massive frame around the bumper pool table situated in the center of the room, gliding round the congested little dance floor adroitly avoiding pool cues and less-talented terpsichoreans.

"Dancing just comes naturally to me," he says. "I've been doing it since I was a teenager. To me, it's basically a release, but I thoroughly enjoy it. I've got a few ladies that I consider extremely good dancers and we pair very well."

How he has the stamina for such release after 12-hour days in the store, hunched over the books in his upstairs office when he's not checking cash registers, stocking shelves, ordering and handling incoming food, and dealing with sundry complaints, remains a mystery.

You can usually locate him in an aisle of the market chatting with friends or listening to and helping to solve some islander's problem.

While the market has been transformed into a modern operation under Michael's auspices, he maintains a friendly, country-store attitude toward customers, most of whom are his friends and neighbors.

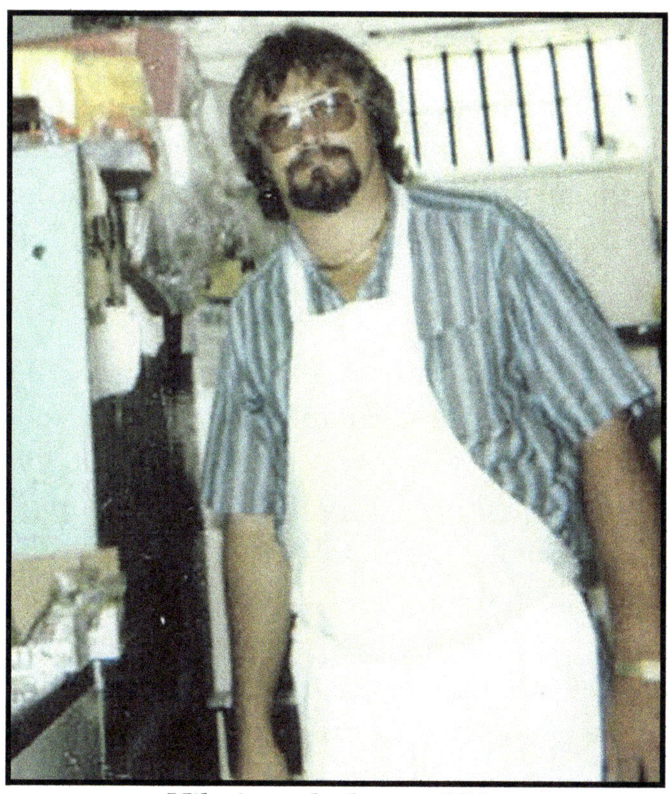

Mike in early days at IGA.

"I'd never let anyone go hungry when I've got food," he says. "There's probably not anybody on the island that, if they were in need, I'd be there to help them if I can. My Dad was the same way. That's just the way I was brought up, to share."

The market was originally established by the Hucks family in 1931. Michael's father's uncle, Joe Hohnerlin, purchased the store shortly thereafter, but groceries were a family business even earlier.

Joe operated a meat market at the corner of Wheaton and Waters Streets in Savannah for years, and Benno worked for Savannah grocers from the time he was a teenager.

In 1934, when Joe had trouble operating the Tybee store, he passed the market to Benno under a gentlemen's agreement. "He gave the store to my father and said when you get the money you can pay me," says Michael.

The original store, located on the front corner of the present property, occupied only about 1,200 square feet, including the apartment in which Benno lived. "It was a little red brick building with gas pumps out front," says Michael, who has examined the ledgers from those early days.

"When Dad took it over, he didn't have enough money to make change for the first dollar he took in. They show that on some days during the winter of 1934 and

1935 he had sales of only 13 cents."

To make matters worse, two other grocery stores opened on the island, but Benno's operation outlasted them both.

"It was hard work and diligence," says Michael of his father's success. "He'd worked for two or three grocers downtown when he was 17 and had become acquainted with Archie Johnson, former president of C&S bank."

It was through this connection that Benno provided a special service for one of the grocers he worked for. "Dad used to go down to the bank every Saturday morning, and Johnson would loan him $6,000. He used the money to cash government checks, mostly from the W.P.A., for farmers who came in for produce."

"There was no collateral on the loan, ever. Mr. Johnson trusted Dad would have the money back. The deal was that when the bank had to close its books at noon, Dad had to have all the money back."

"Dad helped build that grocer's business."

In addition, his father worked at one of the stores all night every Wednesday and Thursday and all day on Friday, sacking up potatoes and onions. "And he'd bag flour in five- and ten-pound bags from the 50-pound bags it used to come in."

"That was back in the days when you had to wait on

every customer. When the customer walked in, he'd walk up to the counter and hand you a list of what he wanted, and you'd go and fill it. That's the way Dad learned the business."

Benno started Tybee's Hosti dynasty when he moved to the island in 1934, and it was Benno's own father who brought the Hosti name to the area from Germany when he immigrated to Georgia and started working as a cop in Savannah.

After the first lean years, Benno made a number of changes to the market, and it became the most popular place to shop for groceries on Tybee.

A roof was built out front to cover fresh produce, an addition was constructed out back, and those gas pumps were eliminated. Then space was added to the side and front, but it was a slow process, a pace which was mostly intentional.

"He didn't want to get any bigger," says Michael. "He was happy with what he had. He was making a good living, and he felt that if he tried to expand, it would cut into his profits. He was happy with a certain level of business."

"It was a glorified convenience store at the time with just a little bit of frozen food and some fresh meat. When I came along, the largest can of anything you could find in the place was a 303 (the standard small can). You couldn't find a two-and-a-half can of anything and nothing bigger than a 12-ounce jar of peanut butter or a ten-ounce jar of jelly."

Once ensconced as manager, Michael started to change things, broadening the scope of the operation to entice more shoppers. He reorganized the interior and exterior of the market in 1982. Included in the changes was a new roof which lowered the temperature inside the store by ten degrees.

Those changes proved a real boon for customers during the island's hot summers, and business at the market increased 300 percent, but what looked like smooth sailing suddenly hit a snag.

While visiting friends in Rochester, N.Y. on his birthday in 1992, Michael learned the store had been struck by lightning during a severe thunderstorm and burned down.

It took 18 months to rebuild the place, part of the delay stemming from a lawsuit filed by a resident behind the proposed new building who claimed it would destroy his already limited view of the ocean two blocks away.

Disheartened, Michael thought about getting out of the grocery business and building condominiums on the property.

Former customers and friends were instrumental in his decision to rebuild. They urged him to reestablish the

Mike starts reconstruction of store after 1992 fire.

store, without which they had to drive to Wilmington to shop.

And the irate neighbor relented, agreeing to drop his suit if Michael could find a buyer for his house (he did, and the house sold in just three days).

Benno never saw the new supermarket. He passed away at age 79 in March of 1994.

Over the years, Michael has developed a keen interest in island history and is privy to numerous nostalgic tidbits. "Most of my friends were a lot older than me, and I listened very well," he says, noting "You can learn a lot if you listen."

"It's amazing what you can learn about who is related to who through marriages and divorces and remarriages and who owned what and how businesses on the island came and went."

"You talk to Edmond Solomon (son of the operator of Tybee's first water system). He's got more knowledge in his head about this place than a set of encyclopedias."

"You learn where the old railroad turntable is down on the south end and the old train station and the bus station and the old parade grounds."

"You learn about the history of the island during World War I and about the Cockspur Island Light House. It's the oldest lighthouse still used as a navigational aid, I think, in the world."

"You learn about Fort Pulaski and how it was built and the damage done to it in the Civil War and how it was done and how many ships are still out there under the water."

"They're still pulling stuff off those ships on the bottom today. We don't see it but the shrimpers do. They'll pull up stuff and take it home. All those anchors you see in yards around the island? They all came off ships anchored offshore, all wooden sailing vessels."

"And there's the gunnery points on the island and the

old watch towers. Most folks never heard of Martello Tower. It was a watch gunnery tower for Fort Pulaski."

"And most folks don't know where the original water tower was. It was in the yard of a little white cottage by Dr. Peterson's house. The foundation is still there."

"There were thousands of snapshots taken of W.P.A. workers building the seawall. A man working for a little paper here at the time took them. They're now in the archives in Atlanta."

"The forms for the sea wall were built right down between 15th and 16th Streets in an open field that was there before the old Brass Rail was built."

"They were mixing concrete by hand in wheelbarrows and buckets and hauling the rocks. The concrete slabs for the walls were moved into place on cannon tracks with a horse pulling them. They'd haul them down the beach and stand 'em up."

"And the stories about the heyday of the old Tybrisa Pavilion and the big-name bands and the people riding out to the island on the train. They'd ride out for the dances in zoot suits, and by the time they got here on that old coal burning train, those damned white suits would be black."

"I remember when they tore up Butler Avenue. It used to be lined with palm trees and oleanders and had a sidewalk on both sides running from one end of it to the other, and I remember when the police cars were 1956 Thunderbirds with knock-off wheels."

"There's all kinds of neat stuff on this island that people don't know the history of."

As to modern times, Michael has some firm opinions on what Tybee needs.

One thing is to modify the island's long standing height restrictions, he says.

"They have to do it to increase the population density. It would bring in large hotels and apartment houses and increase the tax base. With more money they could purchase new fire equipment which would enable the fire department to handle fires in taller buildings."

"It has to happen sometime. If you look around, you won't find more than a hundred vacant lots on the island. The only way to increase the density is to raise building heights."

Though advocating for taller buildings, he remains ecology-minded, believing many island problems stem for "trying to fight Mother Nature."

Nature was causing the island to migrate south toward Little Tybee Island and would have eventually joined the islands had it not been for the dredging of the river channel between them and the construction of the sea wall on the south end, he says.

"Those people on the south end now complain about losing their land to erosion. That never happened before the dredging. Property on the back side of the island would have been building. You used to be able to walk to Little Tybee at low tide."

"You ought to leave Mother Nature alone. Every time you try to fight her, she'll pay you back."

Michael, now 42, says he does not plan to stay in the grocery business forever and hopes to retire by the time he's 55, "although it may take a little longer.

"Despite what most people think, there's not a lot of profit in a grocery store. I actually make a very meager amount, but then it doesn't take much for me to live. I'm by myself, and I don't need a lot."

He received a major financial setback on the same day his father died when he was presented a bill for $28,000 "out of the blue" for work which was not covered by the bank financing he arranged for rebuilding and debt consolidation.

Michael says he is still hustling to cover payments on the note and the increased cost of insurance (his bill is now $30,000 a year) because of the fire.

He also lost a substantial amount of money just after the new store opened because of malfunctioning cash registers which were brought to his attention when a customer checked his bill and found he had been charged only nine cents for a package of coffee.

"I don't know how much I lost," Michael says.

But he figures he'll be over the hump in another 15 months and can then try to put some funds aside for retirement.

"I like south Georgia and the mountains in North Carolina, and I might move to one of those places," he says.

Even if he moves elsewhere, he'll likely spend part of his time on Tybee, however. "Tybee's the only place I've ever lived," he says. "I just love it here. It's different than any other place in the world. I'll probably never leave forever."

Mike relaxes outside his grocery store.

And then there's the family's penchant for politics. "I'd love to have the job of mayor," he says. "I'd love to work for the city, but it wouldn't be fair for me to run now and tell people I'd do a good job. There's not enough time. If I don't have time to take care of what I have to take care of now, how am I going to do a decent job at that?"

Then again, he's reminded that he should have plenty of time if he retires at 55.

"It's something to think about," he says. "If I retire, and I don't leave Tybee I'll seriously consider it."

If all those relatives and friends vote for him, Michael should be a shoo in.

POSTSCRIPT: Michael Hosti did not manage to retire at age 55. He got married not long after this was written and has never left the island. Now well into his 60s, on most days you can still find him hard at work in his grocery store. Most islanders are grateful that he has remained.

George Oliver -
"The Book" Trial Judge Looks Back

Gets Short Shrift in Best Seller

With all the recent hubbub over "THE Book," one key player seems to have been forgotten.

(For those who have been living on another planet, "the book" is John Berendt's best-selling novel Midnight in the Garden of Good and Evil which was set in Savannah, sold over 3 million copies, and remained on the New York Times best-seller list for a record four years.)

But Judge George E. Oliver, who conducted the initial three trials of the book's central character, Jim Williams, is not perturbed by the oversight.

After all, those trials - in which guilty verdicts were overturned twice and one mistrial declared - were just a few of the thousands Oliver has conducted during his more than 40 years of service on the bench and are far from the most important or cherished events in his life.

Oliver, now 83 and still practicing as senior judge of Chatham Superior Court in Savannah, provided a number of extraordinary insights into those trials.

The judge, who is a resident of Tybee Island, has an enviable record as a winner.

He has won all but one of an extended sequence of elections beginning in college; has served as a judge in three area courts; was a World War II sea captain despite the fact that he had no previous experience with ships; has held many of the highest Masonic office; and has maintained a rock-solid marriage for more than 50 years.

Born in Covington, Ga., Oliver's mother passed away shortly after his birth, and his father, a cotton broker, took care of him until he was five, when he moved to Savannah to live with his grandmother and two maiden aunts.

Oliver says his destiny as a Superior Court judge was determined when he was still a tot. "My father told me that as a child my great uncle took me on a tour of a court and gave me a silver dollar when it was over. He said I decided right then that that's where I wanted to be," Oliver smiles.

His first recollection involved another visit to the Savannah court when Judge Peter Meldrum took him on a tour with his grade school class as part of "Boys Week." "I decided during the visit that being a judge on Superior Court was all I ever wanted to be," he says. "I don't ever recall having any other desire."

Fifty years later he was named to a judgeship in the court where he still practices.

After completing two years of high school in Savannah, Oliver attended Belmont Catholic School just outside Charlotte, North Carolina, then graduated from McCallie School in Chattanooga, Tennessee.

"Dr. McCallie told my father 'this young man is rushing out to meet life,'" recalls Oliver of his graduation. "I wanted to go to the University of Georgia, but he suggested a smaller school."

He was registered in The Citadel but "it being a military school, I decided it wasn't for me" and wound up going to Presbyterian College, selecting that over his other option, Davidson, because of its outstanding track team.

"Track was the center of my life at the time," he says. Oliver ran the mile in 4:28, an outstanding time for a high school runner at the time. "High school kids do that regularly now," he says, self-effacingly.

He was a track star with his school team until he was stricken with a severe bone malady which left him hospitalized for almost six months and ultimately required the permanent fusion of four vertebrae in his back.

"It was pretty grim" at the time, he says.

Forced to give up sports following his surgery, Oliver became interested in writing and politics and ran for election as editor of his college magazine while at Presbyterian. His principal opponent advised him to drop out of the race because none of the freshman class - the school's biggest block of voters - knew him, hence "You have no way of winning."

The opponent promised to appoint Oliver to the magazine staff once he, himself, was elected. Oliver told his self-confident school mate he still intended to run and felt it might be a distinct advantage that the freshmen didn't know him "since they do know you!"

Proving his political prowess early, the judge won that first election handily.

Later, he received his law degree from the University of Georgia, where he maintained his winning streak by being elected vice president of his junior class and president of his senior class.

It's not those electoral successes but his unsuccessful attempt to assist a fellow law student that he remembers most vividly.

"He came to school with the only two shirts he owned in a carpetbag," recalls the judge. "I'd always heard about them, but it was the first carpetbag I'd ever seen."

The student got through his freshman year but started struggling with grades in his sophomore year and was told he would have to leave. Oliver took up his cause, going to the dean to say he shouldn't drop the boy "because this was a different situation."

The dean was adamant in insisting that the standard grade point average had to be maintained with no exceptions. Oliver reminded him that the lad's father was now a federal judge and "he didn't burn this place up" with terrific grades.

Then he asked the dean if the boy's father's affiliation with a popular fraternity had anything to do with him being permitted to stay in school.

"At that point the dean said 'Mr. Oliver, this conference is over. You're excused'!"

The boy eventually graduated from Mercer College, became a Superior Court judge and provided Oliver with the last laugh. Oliver took great pleasure in re-introducing the former student, then a judge, to his former dean during a Bar Association gathering.

Oliver joined the Savannah law firm of Kennedy and Kennedy following his graduation and remained there until the outbreak of World War II, when he attempted to enlist in the regular military nine times but was declared 4-F because of his back problems.

"I finally went to the Coast Guard," he says. "I told

them I didn't want to spend the rest of my life explaining why I wasn't in the war if I wasn't dragging my leg."

A local medical examining officer said there was no way he could get in but told him he could drive to Charleston to apply anyway, noting "at the least I would have a nice drive over. The next time I saw a doctor I was serving aboard a ship in the Caribbean."

Oliver, who had never been aboard a ship of any kind, was assigned as an officer aboard a Coast Guard cutter.

To his surprise and initial chagrin, he was named skipper when the captain took command of another vessel and said, simply: "Ensign Oliver, it's your ship!"

Suddenly he was in charge of the cutter and its crew of 50 men and four officers but "we learned to live with it," he laughs. "The quartermaster at the wheel told me to 'never give it a thought. Between you and myself we can take this vessel anywhere.'"

Oliver admits he was terrified but managed to handle the ship, albeit bumping it around a bit when coming into docks.

He remembers that his chief engineer, a warrant officer, told him "If you'll quit ringing those damned bells, I'll fit it into the dock."

Oliver skippered the ship for nine months in the Dutch

Judge George E. Oliver.

West Indies, which was a critically important area at the time with a hotbed of German submarine activity because of nearby oil refineries supplying gasoline to England.

Oliver laughs when he remembers receiving a letter from his father saying he was glad his son was safe sailing about the Caribbean. It arrived the same day a ship near his was torpedoed and sunk.

Following that assignment, he was placed in charge of a freighter in the Pacific for the remainder of the war.

Between those assignments Oliver returned to Savannah to marry Dorothy Cornell, whom he had met in a Sunday School Class years earlier. She was the daughter of John Cornell, then president of Savannah Bank and Trust, who had been on Georgia Governor Eugene Talmadge's staff and was a Chatham County commissioner.

The marriage got off to a somewhat shaky start since Oliver opposed Talmadge, was on the opposite side of litigation with the county commission, and kept his bank account at the Citizens and Southern Bank.

"The only thing we had in common is that we were Methodists and Masons and we both loved his daughter," laughs Oliver.

But none of this deterred them. The judge and Dorothy have now been married for 53 years.

Perhaps, he reflects, it is because prior to his own marriage he had never lived in a home with anyone who was married, hence never had inappropriate role models.

"One thing I've learned about marriage is that, when you're married, there is no court of appeal," he says, somewhat sardonically.

The closest call he had on his Pacific tour occurred when his vessel was approached by a Liberty ship during the invasion of Palawan.

"We were in a convoy as part of the landing when somebody came and got me out of my bunk. I ran topside in my underwear. I remember being as cold as I've ever been in my life, and there was a Liberty ship coming down on us. There was a blackout, and we couldn't turn on our lights to signal, and it looked as big as a house."

"I was hoping he knew more about operating a ship than I did. It missed us by just 20 feet!"

Oliver says he has done no boating since his wartime

experience.

"I don't even go fishing," he chuckles.

Following the war, the judge rejoined the Kennedy law firm before becoming a law partner with Malberry Smith. It was about this time that he made his only unsuccessful bid for office, when he ran for a seat in the Georgia State Legislature.

"I was soundly defeated," he laughs. "I realized the people in the community wanted me far more here than in Atlanta and I'd better practice law and forget about politics."

Shortly after his unsuccessful run, his father passed away.

"He called me in just before he died to tell me he was proud of me, that I had done everything he expected."

Then his father admonished him to take care of his aunts since they had cared for him when he was young and said the only thing Oliver had ever done to disappoint him was failing to resume his activities in his Masonic lodge after World War II. (The judge had joined the Masons when he was 22 but lost interest "because ceremony doesn't much appeal to me.")

Those words had a lasting impact. Shortly after his death, Oliver became hyperactive in that organization.

He became a member of the Scottish Rite Bodies, York Rite Bodies, Red Cross of Constantine and Cabiri, and was named director of Jesters and Potentate of Alee Temple of the Shrine, Master of Landrum Lodge in Savannah, Junior Grand Warden for the Grand Lodge of Georgia, and, in 1972, Grand Master of Georgia's Ancient and Accepted Scottish Rite of Free Masonry.

He also changed his mind about politics and, in 1955, ran for and was elected judge of Recorder's Court, where he served for two terms before being elected as a State Court judge.

Shortly thereafter his childhood dream came true.

In 1970, Governor Lester Maddox called to say he was considering appointing him to fill a vacancy on Superior Court, even though Maddox was well aware Oliver had not supported him politically.

Oliver, who concedes that his activities as a Mason did not hurt him, remembers that call quite well.

"When he called me up, he said 'Pote - I know you've been Potentate of the Shrine Club - you want to be judge of the Superior Court?'

"I said: 'Governor, in the worst way!'

"Then he asked if he appointed me, could I be elected when the term expired. I said yes and then he asked if I would come to Atlanta to be sworn in. But after I agreed he said, 'How about raising me a crowd in Savannah, and I'll come down there'."

Oliver did, indeed, raise a crowd.

"The courtroom was full, and there were people standing outside," he recalls.

Judge Oliver has repeatedly won reelection since his 1970 appointment. He was designated Chief Judge of Chatham Superior Court in 1976, remaining in that position until being named Senior Judge.

He says fulfilling his childhood dream is everything he anticipated.

"I have gone to work with a song in my heart every day, happy that I could practice law and happy that I could be a judge," he says.

He has no plans to relinquish his present position, which requires his presence in court once a week to take pleas which have been agreed upon by the district attorney and attorneys for the defendants, rule on probation violations, and preside at "trials that no one else wants," he grins.

Oliver also has jurisdiction to sit on the bench anywhere in the state.

Since his move to Tybee, the judge must now make a weekly 20-mile trek to Savannah, but he feels it's worth it.

"No married man should be without a place to go," he observes, judiciously.

Besides, he says, "I love the island, the people, and the ocean. I love walking on the beach. It's different from any other beach."

"And," he grins, "I've become one of the world's greatest connoisseurs of bikinis."

The judge feels he has a slight advantage over some since his wife does not accompany him on such strolls because she is prone to sunburn.

To maintain his pleasant life at the beach, that's one thing the judge says he's "sworn" to himself: "I'll never get another sunburn."

POSTSCRIPT: Judge Oliver died on July 2, 2004, after a long illness. He was 89.

Marlyce Kling - Circuitous Route Leads to Tybee

Writer Finds Peace Beside The Ocean

She's come a long way, geographically, from her life-long, land-locked home in Iowa... and even further, philosophically, to reach her present state of euphoria.

"I'm happier now than I've ever been in my life," she says, smiling serenely.

It's easier than poking your toe in the sand to believe Marlyce Kling.

She's either a consummate actress or the genuine article, reveling in the joy of living and willing to risk the emotional pain of relationships gone awry because she cares about everyone and refuses to miss any opportunity to find new friends.

"I really understand the preciousness of time, and I understand the preciousness of every encounter - every phone call, even with people I will never see," she says.

"I really understand about ships in the night and that

this may be your only shot. While I don't make perfect decisions all the time, I take the chance."

Marlyce is a teacher, counselor, and poet who, while a professed student of Eastern religions, is deeply devoted to the traditional Christian church.

She is disarmingly, often disconcertingly, honest, a pleasantly eclectic mix made the more unusual by the fact that she was once a hard-nosed journalist specializing in ferreting out sometimes seamy scandals.

Marlyce did not come to her present, comfortable station in life by prancing lightly down a primrose path.

Her route was navigated with the compass of spiritual study when it became almost impossible because of the loss of both her 18-year-old son and her 51-year-old husband in what she says was an idyllic marriage.

She made the final passage to what she views as her seaside paradise on Tybee grudgingly, at the urging of another son who apparently knew her better than she knew herself.

Born and bred in Iowa, Marlyce was attending Buena Vista College in Storm Lake, Iowa, when she was first married.

That was apparently not a marriage made in heaven. Marlyce will only admit that she was "very young and the marriage was brief." The best part of the union was that it produced her two sons, Chuck and Brad. Following its demise, she began teaching creative writing in Osage, Iowa, where she met Keith, an electrical engineer who became her husband for the next 23 years, and her still-persistent poetic muse.

Taking a break to reflect on island life.

Soon after their marriage, they acquired a cabin on an island in the Mississippi River, near the tiny town of McGregor, population 900.

Marlyce says that area is the most beautiful in Iowa and they visited their cabin as often as possible "and every time we went there, we hated to go home."

One of the many pleasant aspects of those trips was visiting a little newspaper in McGregor, the weekly North Iowa Times, which was founded in 1856 and was the oldest newspaper in the state.

She got to know the editor but "the paper wasn't much," she recalls. "They just weren't doing it right, and he said the only big story he had come across in years was when the bridge washed out!"

Still, she felt an affinity for the little weekly and on one of those visits told Keith she would "give anything to own that paper."

Those reluctant return trips home became unnecessary when Keith presented her with the newspaper as a birthday present.

Marlyce, who had worked for the Storm Lake Register and Pilot Tribune while in college, hence knew the pressure of newspapering first hand, said her initial response was: "Are you crazy!?"

But she realized running the paper would fulfill their dream of living in the area (which they wound up doing, in a cabin on their 200-acre island for 14 years before moving six miles away to Monona), and accepted the gift after holding a bargaining session to establish ground rules.

Marlyce says she and Keith "were always really good at bargains - that's the reason our marriage was so successful, we had both had failed marriages, and we weren't going through that again - ours was a 'no exit' marriage. No one was going to stand and argue with anyone. When we had problems, we just went at them and solved them."

The rules were straight forward, stringent, and not a little one-sided.

"I will be the editor, and I will have absolute control over every word that is printed," she insisted. "You will have absolutely no say, and I will only promise that you will not be sued for libel."

After a bit of give and take, they did agree that Keith would have absolute control of publishing, finances, and advertising.

"And that," she smiles, "is the way we did it."

Given her penchant for truthful but frequently unpopular stories, Marlyce was amazed at how well Keith handled his end of the bargain, recalling irate readers who descended on him in the office demanding: "Can't you control your wife?" to which he invariably responded that he had "no desire to control her since she was right!"

"He always stood behind me, and we uncovered embezzlement, broke open closed-door school board meetings, uncovered a corrupt election which listed voters who were dead...it just went on and on," she says. "I cost him a lot of advertising, but he didn't care. He was the most ethical, principled man I have ever met."

While her job was arduous, including everything from writing the lead story and about 50 percent of every issue to typesetting intricate and time-consuming legal advertising, she thrived on the work.

"We just had a wonderful time," she says.

When they sold the newspaper seven years later,

Marlyce discovered that though readers "would cuss us out and rant about it, they really believed it, and we found we had a lot of people out there rooting for us. Honest to God, I found out there is a silent majority!"

The paper grew from its original eight pages to 24; circulation jumped from 500 to 2,000 in a county with a total population of 10,000, and they made a substantial profit on its sale.

There life in McGregor was not without tragedy, however.

It was there that she lost her 18-year-old son, Chuck, shortly after taking over the newspaper.

Chuck, who Marlyce has since concluded was probably suffering from manic-depression, attended a party one night during which he told friends he planned to take his own life.

Chuck didn't drink at that party and his friends "thought they had talked him out of it," she says.

After the party, he drove to a railroad crossing, and straddled it with his car, leaving the engine running and the headlights on.

Marlyce says the engineer of an approaching train spotted the lights and "laid on his whistle and brakes, doing everything he could," and at the last possible moment her son sped off the tracks.

The engineer, who later informed her that this type of suicide is not rare, and his train had hit and killed at least one other person, was relieved, but his relief was short-lived.

Her son drove to the far side of a nearby curve in the tracks, this time parking across them with his engine and lights turned off, and it was there that the train killed him.

"That must have been horrible for the engineer," says Marlyce. "He had to kill Chuck twice."

Marlyce, herself, was devastated by her son's death.

"My grief over Chuck was so deep, and I hadn't organized my thoughts properly," she says. "I just talked about it all the time."

Seeking solace and closure, she studied Eastern religions which she credits with "the way I conduct my life now - the cycle of things - why I'm seldom ruffled, and I understand the world from my point of view."

"I was determined to get over it. It took me a long time to get over his death, but I think that [her study of religions] is the reason I survived my son's death as well as I have. I am very, very, very happy because I choose to be happy."

Always religious, Marlyce was affiliated with the Lutheran Church for most of her life, and says she is about to join the Episcopal Church on Tybee, though "I've been going to the Catholic Church and the Island's Christian Church, and I love them both."

It was her study of Taoism, however, that she credits most for helping her through the crisis of her son's death. "I think you have to regain your balance, and I think the truth of it is that my study of Taoism helped immensely," she says.

Marlyce finds joy in her garden.

Many of Marlyce's most peaceful hours were spent in her gardens on the island in Iowa and later in Monona, where she grew not only flowers and herbs but virtually all the family's vegetables.

Two years ago, she says she was "sitting on my knees in my garden, and I had never been happier in my life, and ten days later my world was absolutely turned upside down."

Keith came home saying he thought he had a touch of the flu "but he was all yellow, and I was sure he had hepatitis," she recalls.

Despite his discomfort, they drove to a football game where their daughter was a cheerleader only to find that Keith couldn't get out of the car when they parked for the game.

Marlyce drove him to his doctor and "he took one look at Keith and sent him to the hospital," she says. "They told us Keith had cancer in every part of his body."

Ten days later, Keith was dead.

He had been in an automobile accident in which he cracked a vertebra in his lower back a year earlier, and he had continued to suffer back pain, but they attributed it to the injury, according to Marlyce.

We were so stupid and just so anti-doctors, and he was one of those people who never complained," she says. "He thought you just lived with pain, and you just shake it off."

In her grief following his death Marlyce says "I just kept saying to myself all is impermanent - all is without self. These are the facts."

"I told myself I didn't die, praise God. I did not die even though I felt like I had."

"When my son died, I felt like I died, and it took so

many years to feel whole again. I didn't want to waste that time. I understand the preciousness of time."

She busied herself settling family affairs and gardening for a year following her husband's death while holding frequent phone conversations with her son, Brad, who was living on Tybee.

Marlyce reassured him that she was doing fine, but Brad urged her to join him on the island.

"Brad just knew me so well, and he knew what kind of people I'd be interested in," she says. "I really had to dig to find interesting people for intellectual stimulation in Iowa."

Marlyce heads out on her bike.

"But I fought so terribly coming to Tybee because I had lived in my house for 14 years and was so comfortable there, and I hated to part with my gardens. They were the things I was sorriest to leave."

Ultimately, however, Marlyce moved to the island last February, and now considers the move one of the best decisions she ever made.

"Here I get to have it all!" she exclaims. "I get to be on vacation. I have the ocean, and I get all these people for very little cost."

"The days are so full, and I'm so thrilled by the inclusion. I feel so included! I've never had so much wonderful conversation as I've had on Tybee, and that's my number one entertainment. The philosophical diversity here is awesome."

"I feel like they've let me in the game! I'm no longer on the bench. Keith would have loved it. We would have laughed ourselves sick here!"

Just prior to her departure from Iowa, Marlyce published a book of poetry entitled Atlanta Constance Sampson and Other Poems.

The book is a tribute to Sampson, who was an artist and a resident of Monona who painted for most of her life but waited until she was 91 to receive recognition and achieve her dream of having a one-woman show at the National Arts Club in New York.

On the back cover of her book, Marlyce wrote: "She's my hero. She never gave up, eating little, living in one-room, and painting on both sides of the canvas or brown paper bag."

Like her artist heroine, Marlyce has never given up.

"Pain is an emotion, so I might as well use it to my

advantage and, hopefully, I'll be able to chuck it relatively quickly," she says. "You just take your turn, see what there's left to do, and do the best you can."

"Love and service. That's all there is. If you keep it simple, you really can do quite a bit. I'm feeling like I have a lot to say right now."

Since her arrival on the island, Marlyce has done considerably more than just "a bit." Her production of poetry, much of it with traces of Eastern philosophy, has been prolific and she has immersed herself in Yoga.

"Between Yoga and the ocean, I've really got my feet on the ground, and I'm so very grateful to the Tybee Arts Association. I have learned so much and met so many wonderful people."

"Can you imagine all the artists and musicians? I meet someone almost every day - a writer or some other interesting person. One day I met a Persian rug restorer (Tony Scarwid), and I couldn't get over it. Isn't that unbelievable - a Persian rug restorer on Tybee Island? I just thought I'm in the right place."

A strong believer in physical fitness, Marlyce works out three days a week at the YMCA, and, next to Yoga, she most enjoys riding her bicycle on the beach every day.

"That's my dearest activity," she says.

Marlyce creates on computer.

She has also written two novels and a pair of screenplays she hopes to market and is collaborating with two other island women on plans to create a publishing firm to produce a series of books about Tybee.

Meanwhile, she keeps busy gardening again, although she admits her green thumb has proven less successful in the island's sand than it was in Iowa.

In her spare time, she counsels troubled people, many of them youngsters "who just seem to find me," she says.

She's also taken a "regular job" handling the leasing of apartments, houses, and condos which she says provides "needed structure in my life. I'm grateful for it, and it helps pay the rent."

It's been a long and difficult journey, but Marlyce has finally found a safe haven.

"If I won the lottery, and it was stipulated that I had to move back to Iowa, I would decline," she says. "I am mad for Tybee. I've never felt more calm. I've never been happier."

POSTSCRIPT: After Marlyce discovered Doc's Bar on Tybee's south end, she spent considerable time there in the evening meeting what was then its eclectic assortment of customers. During those visits she sat at a corner table writing most of her book entitled Tybee Island, the Republic of Love. Among those she met was Edgar Johnson, a visitor from Atlanta. While she did not win the lottery, Marlyce did win Edgar's heart. They married and moved to Stone Mountain, Ga. where they continue to live, hopefully pain-free, and indulging in intellectual conversation. Marlyce says one of the few things they don't discuss, at least since the 2020 presidential election, is politics because they, like the country as a whole, have distinctly different views on this topic. Meanwhile, they seem to be doing the best they can.

Bob Martin -
Old Vet Remains Ready to Serve

Worldwide Adventures Started Early

What do you do if you've retired after 23 years of "ultra" active military service?

Service which left you 100 percent disabled and walking with the assistance of a cane?

And then, when you're 60 years-old, you're notified to report for active war duty?

That's what happened to Tybee's Bob Martin - a decorated but battered veteran of shooting wars and high intrigue in super-cold, cold, and semi-cold wars - at the outset of the Persian Gulf War.

If you're Bob Martin, what you do, after a momentary pause for disbelief, is start packing your bags to head for another one.

Bob, who had retired as a warrant officer 20 years earlier, was ordered to report for duty within 24 hours to

Ft. Belvoir, Virginia, and never one to question orders, was preparing to make the trip.

His wife, Fran, was also packing her things in case she was permitted to accompany him to his new assignment.

They were spared the trauma just as Bob headed for Hunter Field for his vouchers and uniforms when the brief war ended.

Saddam Hussein should thank his lucky stars.

Bob, a parachutist, demolitions expert, designer of special mine fuses, mechanic, engineer, and specialist in surreptitious assignments, was a real handful when he was in the military.

But when he received those short-lived orders, he was relaxing on Tybee, a home boy come home, devoting his waning years to holding his battered body together and helping others like himself.

Between visits to veteran's hospitals to be treated for service-related injuries (Bob has back and neck injuries, problems with his extremities, hearing impairment and, 25 years after the fact, was determined to have lung damage stemming from exposure to Agent Orange), he and Fran ferry other vets to hospitals and provide support for Tybee area residents.

While ailing and rail thin, Bob has a quick and infectious grin, and enjoys his afternoon beer. His cap, adorned with service ribbons (including his father's old Corps of Engineers pin representing 41 years' meritorious service), is an omnipresent part of his attire.

Even as a kid before entering the service at age 17, Bob was a handful. "I was always getting in fights with other boys in public schools," he recalls.

It got so bad that his parents and school officials agreed it was best that he transfer to Benedictine Military Academy "to get some discipline."

But don't blame it all on Bob. He came by his feisty nature naturally.

His mother, Rebecca, was nicknamed "Two-Gun Becky" after she spotted a Peeping Tom on a ladder at the window of her daughters' bedroom. She snatched the intruder's shirt right off his back, grabbed a gun and blazed away as he scampered back down the ladder.

"Ma thought she'd killed the guy when he fell to the ground," says Bob. Turns out she did nearly scare him to death, but his sudden fall was actually caused when a clothesline caught him at the neck as he ran.

"Ma's shots hit near his feet," says Bob. "He escaped with his life when she woke me to tell me she'd just killed a man."

That wasn't the only armed incident involving "Two-Gun Becky."

When Bob was ten, he got in another of those fights with a neighborhood boy, and the kid's father didn't take it too kindly. "He came to our house to beat me," says Bob.

His mother, who had suffered a stroke and was in a wheelchair at the time, had a different idea, however. She trundled her chair out to the porch and confronted the man with her gun.

"You just go on home, and when my husband gets back, he'll bring Bob over, and y'all can decide who started what," she said. "If Bob's at fault, his father will take care of spanking him, but you're not gonna do it."

Later, his dad hauled him over to the man's house to get to the bottom of the fracas, but the man made the mistake of greeting them with the salutation: "Well, I see you finally brought the little S.O.B. over here," says Bob, adding, "Dad whipped the guy, and they both went to jail."

He was saved in another fight by his sister.

According to Bob, she hit Jack Youmans (now a Tybee city councilman) with a rake when he came over to join a fight Bob was engaged in with Jack's brother.

"We were a real close family," Bob smiles.

Benedictine didn't do all that was expected for him, and Bob informed his father he was dropping out to look for a job.

His father, who was a dredge captain with the Corps of Engineers in charge of maintaining the intracoastal waterway from North Carolina to Florida and the Savannah River from the Houlihan Bridge to its mouth, told him to forget about finding work because he had a job for him.

"He put me on a contract pipeline dredge in the marsh, rolling 30-inch steel pipe. Then I became a winchman on the pipe and operated a dredge tender. We were working 12-hour shifts. I had the one from six at night 'til six in the morning to keep me out of trouble."

His father apparently had the right idea. "At the end of that summer I was ready to go back to school," Bob confesses.

His childhood wasn't all fights and work, however.

He remembers his first joy-filled visits to Tybee, riding the old train to the beach as a 2-year-old on outings with his family.

Later, he came out on weekends, sleeping and cavorting through long summer nights under the old Tybrisa Pavilion, "drinking some with the other kids, but never getting into real trouble."

He also spent time with his father on the dredge runs, getting off on barrier islands learning to fish and hunt, love nature and become self-reliant.

Bob hunted on Little St. Simon's Island before it was turned into a protected preserve. "I got a boar there with 9-inch tusks; dressed out at 470 pounds," he recalls, also noting that he shot a 16-point deer weighing in at 270 pounds.

His father sent him to Daufuskie Island to live a while with his cabin boy's family. It was there that Bob learned to smoke fish and oysters, salt shrimp, and generally live off the land.

He also learned to gather pineapple pears on the island for his mother. "She loved them better than anything," he says.

When he turned 13, his father gave him an old wooden bateau he had found on an island after a hurricane and launched him on the water at Causton Bluff. "I took off with three sandwiches and three quarts of water and rowed that thing around Skidaway Island down to Hayners Creek, 25 miles away," recalls Bob. "The water and the sandwiches were gone when I got there."

And Bob's father often brought animals he found on the islands back to their home in Savannah.

Once, he brought a raccoon that the family adopted, naming it Clark Gable. The animal weighed 35 pounds when it was run over by a streetcar. He also brought rabbits which they placed in a cage, but they soon overran the place. "We hauled them down to Bonaventure Cemetery and let them out, but they hopped along right behind us when we headed back," Bob laughs. "They finally scattered when a streetcar approached."

"He brought in a couple of goats once," says Bob. "We got rid of 'em when they went under the house and started a ruckus at 3 a.m. and Mom had to crawl under there in her nightgown to get 'em out."

When his dad brought some pigeons home, Bob decided to start his own business raising and selling them. "I got a contract to supply fresh squab to the old DeSoto Hotel, but I had to give it up when my sister started naming the darned things. She raised a fit when I was ready to haul them off to the hotel."

He managed to make spending money catching and selling fish and gathering turtle eggs from the beach, selling the latter for 2 cents apiece to bars in Savannah. "The drinkers used to love to crack them there at the bar, suck 'em out, and then swallow a drink," says Bob. "Of course, I'd never do anything like that now."

He also joined other young boys as Coast Watchers, walking the beach on Tybee during World War II, looking out for German submarines.

He was there in 1944 when a German sub, waiting for ships to sail from the Savannah port, was sunk just offshore by a U.S. blimp from the Glencoe Naval Station. "When they blew it up, bread wrappers from a Savannah bakery floated on the surface, proving the Germans were getting supplies from the area," he says.

Bob joined the Army and headed to Ft. Jackson, South Carolina, for basic training in 1947, when he was 17. He was named squad leader immediately because of his high school military training.

After basic, Bob went through jump school at Ft. Benning, Georgia, then was transferred to Aberdeen Proving Grounds in Maryland for training as an automotive track vehicle repairman.

Following training, he was shipped to Adak in the Aleutian Islands to clean up ammunition depots left in disarray there after World War II. "I was there for nine months when the Korean War broke out," says Bob, who was now a sergeant.

"Then they took me and sent me to Anchorage, Alaska, to build a railroad" for shipment of atomic weapons to Elmendorf Air Force Base. "We mounted a jet engine on the back of a two-and-a-half-ton truck to melt the permafrost to lay the rails."

Later, he maintained trucks and cleared roads from Fairbanks to the Canadian border to enable the hauling of material to ships heading for Korea.

Whatever his assignment, he always got in a little hunting on the side. "Got me a moose and a brown bear in Alaska," he says.

Bob Martin relaxes in his home on Lewis Ave.

It was about this time that Bob made plans to marry that high-school sweetheart with whom he had corresponded from the time he enlisted.

But immediately after their wedding was scheduled to take place in Savannah, he got orders to report to Korea.

Georgia Senator Richard Russell intervened to make the wedding possible, according to Bob, who says "with political influence now marked on my record, I was put on a B-25 bomber as tail gunner and flown from Alaska to Oklahoma City; then on a C-47 for the flight to Georgia, still filthy from working in the shop and still wearing my arctic gear."

Following the wedding, he was assigned to an engineer regiment in San Pedro, California, promoted to first sergeant of his battalion and shipped to Panama to help build an amphibious training station and a jungle warfare training center.

Bob stayed there for more than three years, before finally being shipped home on a transport ship with Prince, a dog he adopted during his lengthy assignment.

Just after arriving stateside at a dock in Brooklyn, he was almost arrested. Prince, who had undergone what must have been exceptionally effective house training, had refused to relieve himself for the entire five-day voyage and quickly used "the only tree in the entire area" to do his business.

His "business" was very large, and Brooklyn authorities took a dim view of the affront to their sparse tree population. It was only after an extended plea and explanation that Bob was able to convince police to overlook the transgression.

Now a warrant officer, Bob was sent to Ft. Belvoir, where his commanding officer offered him the choice of being shipped to Korea or accompanying him on his next assignment with the Arctic Task Force.

He opted for the task force assignment, helping build a ballistic missile warning facility in Greenland, since it was supposed to enable him to return stateside each winter to spend time with his family.

Assigned as "swing commander" in charge of a group of huge, specially constructed tractors, Bob pulled sleds loaded with 20 tons of equipment from Tule, Greenland to the construction site on an ice cap 280 miles to the north, travelling at a speedy three miles per hour.

Bob got in a little hunting on one of the trips, but this time it was inadvertent. A polar bear followed the procession from Tule, eating scraps from each camp site as they moved on, then got ravenous when they started their return trip, and the scraps were gone.

The bear attacked the convoy, and Bob, armed with the only weapon in the group, an M-1 rifle with eight rounds of ammunition, had to shoot the animal.

He says he hit it with all eight shots, the first from a distance of 50 yards. The bear was 15 feet away when it finally dropped. "The bear measured 13 feet from paw to paw," says Bob.

After the first summer, he was looking forward to spending the winter with his family at Ft. Belvoir, but three days after his arrival he was sent to Switzerland for special training on snow blowing equipment used for clearing avalanches.

The Greenland station was to be embedded in the ice cap, under snow which had to be cleared before the necessary trenches could be dug in the cap.

That summer Bob was back in Greenland in "white-out" weather, where he says ice crystals were so thick in the air you could see nothing and often became disoriented. Metal foil had to be placed on poles marking their route, and radar was used to spot these in order to proceed.

A point person, tethered to a tractor by a rope, had to lead the procession through crevasse fields to prevent the entire group from falling through the deep, snow-covered openings.

That was Bob's job.

He says he only fell into a crevasse once, dropping 75 feet and dangling on the end of the rope while being banged against the sides of the crevasse for five hours before the team could pull him back up. He suffered frostbite on his fingers and feet during the ordeal.

After construction was completed that summer, Bob figured he'd have a chance to take it easy for a change only to learn that when the job was over, it wasn't over.

The government decided to build the world's largest ice-bound fuel storage area in the ice cap and figured Bob was the man to spearhead the effort. He was sent to West Virginia to learn to use a coal-mining machine to tunnel into solid ice where a huge pit would be cleared to hold the fuel.

When he returned to the Arctic the following summer, it was the International Geophysical Year, and Bob was assigned to look after a group of professors, or "over-educated idiots" as he described them.

The professors knew about white outs - "they'd studied them and read about them, but had absolutely no experience with them," he says - and they kept wandering about and getting lost.

Bob issued orders saying no one was to leave their huts without a lifeline, but the professors paid no attention, and he had to risk his own men's lives searching for them.

"I finally had to lock 'em in and station Koski, a huge Eskimo, at the door to make sure they didn't get out," he says. "Koski weighed about 280 pounds."

Nobody got out.

His third summer followed the same pattern. Bob was sent to Houghton, Michigan, to develop a waterproof mine fuse to replace the ones used in Europe which froze in the winter, enabling tanks to run over them without exploding.

His team solved the fuse problem by using Teflon coating.

When that job was completed, he was ordered to France to work with a communications zone engineer and was placed in something he says was somewhat spuriously called "installations management and doing whatever I had to do."

Then he was zigged to Germany to work with "special" signal people and zagged to Turkey where he was ordered to install a solar battery-powered radio relay station atop Mt. Ararat as a listening device to monitor Russian communications.

While climbing Mt. Ararat, Bob claims he saw the remains of Noah's Ark, "part of it down in a glacier and the other part up on the mountain. It had little cubicles in it, like animal compartments. It was the real thing!"

His conclusion was confirmed two weeks later when Fran turned on TV's Discovery Channel and saw pictures of the structure "exactly as I had described it in my conversation with her."

From Turkey Bob was routed to Libya just after Muammar Khadafy took power.

Posing as a surplus arms buyer, he took four men in to immobilize the huge stock of U.S. equipment in the area, making it useless to the new dictator. After wiring the major pieces with explosives and time delay fuses, Bob says "we were in the air and out of there before it blew. I don't know if anybody was hurt or not, but Khadafy didn't get any of that stuff."

"After that, I was all over. I worked with the Greek Army and the Turkish Army and with any NATO country that was using our equipment. I'd train 'em and show 'em how to repair it."

"Then we came back to the States, and I was going to go on jump status for the first time at Ft. Bragg, North Carolina."

He says he and his wife were in their house for only four days "when the Cuban Missile Crisis hit." Bob says he and a dozen men were sent "in there in something I can't talk about."

When the crisis passed, he was pulled back to an area in south Florida, between Miami and Homestead, where "the army had set up missiles all over." He says his unit was placed in a three-story potato packing warehouse and "we stayed in the compound, away from the public, for five months."

Finally, Bob was given a permanent change of station and his family was permitted to come down. "They told me I would be there three years, and I bought a house. We were in the house for seven months when the colonel called me in and said 'Mr. Martin, you have orders.'

I asked where in the hell am I going now, and he said Okinawa."

A typhoon hit the island shortly after his arrival in 1963, and he was evacuated from his house at 4 a.m. just before his house was washed away, sliding down a hill.

While on the island he headed a group charged with

blowing open the entrance to what was called the Cave of the Virgins.

The cave had been sealed in the Battle for Okinawa, trapping Japanese soldiers inside, and Bob's work enabled the Japanese to recover the bodies.

When his family was finally permitted to join him on Okinawa, they arrived on a Tuesday. The following Thursday Bob was shipped to Vietnam.

He served as an advisor there for eight months in Vietnam, although his duty station remained listed as Okinawa, and after his three-year tour on Okinawa ended, "they said you haven't been to Vietnam yet. That's where you're going."

Bob returned to that war in 1967 and with 18 days left on his tour there, he was caught in the Tet Offensive. The BOQ beside the racetrack in Saigon where he was lodged was surrounded - "our Vietnamese guards were shooting at us," he says.

His group was trapped for seven days with food and ammunition being supplied by helicopter. "I was damned glad to get out of there," he says.

When they finally hauled him out, Bob had compressed vertebra in his neck and other injuries and wound up in a VA hospital for more than two years. By the time he was released, the Army had taken over Hunter Army Airfield, and Bob was assigned there as post engineer until 1969, when he decided to leave military service.

Once his mind and body had recovered somewhat, Bob went to work as purchasing agent, equipment foreman, and supervisor for a shipping company in Savannah.

Then he opened his own business selling, renting, and maintaining forklifts with a partner from Atlanta, until the company folded when he and his partner had a falling out.

That's when Bob retired for good, moving to his long-cherished island of Tybee.

During their 12 years on the island, he and Fran have kept active helping other veterans. Bob also spends time improving their house, working with the VFW and his DAV chapter where he has served as commander.

They did leave the island to make one long trip, 3,700 miles travelling through Arkansas and up through Canada, returning along the East Coast and Outer Banks of North Carolina. It ended in another near disaster when Bob collapsed with a perforated intestine caused by a fish bone he swallowed.

Peritonitis set in, and Bob was hospitalized for longer than might have been necessary when a nurse forgot to deflate a catheter when removing it and the inflated portion broke off inside him.

Although his body has suffered amazing abuse over the years, Bob is doing better now. He sipped a few and was in good spirits at his 66th birthday celebration on Oct. 11.

He looked as though he might be almost ready to check his mail again.

Who knows? The military might need a good man, and Bob could have his bags packed on short notice.

POSTSCRIPT: Robert C. "Bob" Martin passed away at home on Tybee April 17, 2008. He was 77 years old. His widow, Frances "Fran" Gammon Martin, was 74 when she died in their island home on July 4, 2016.

Mike Ryan -
Developer Changing Face of Island

Believes Condos Pose No Threat

Mike Ryan

He may have been most instrumental in changing the face of Tybee over its last four frenetic years of growth.

Mike Ryan conceived and constructed the first of what is now a plethora of condominiums in the commercial area on the south end of the island. His seventh such structure is now nearing completion in the same block as the first he erected three years ago at the corner of Strand Avenue and T.S. Chu. It will bring the total number of individual condo units he has created to 46.

All six units in his new building have already been sold, with prices ranging from $289,000 to $319,000. In his initial condominium, units were priced from $180,000 to $210,000.

His buildings, some of which have replaced familiar old beach houses, are high profile and have become somewhat controversial.

Mike, himself, is neither.

He is a low keyed, infectiously gregarious man who has a genuine love for the island.

Originally from Savannah (his father was police chief there at one time), he attended Benedictine Military Academy and Armstrong College. He has been coming to the beach since he was a tot and remembers the live music on the old pier and the Brass Rail and bowling alleys "when 16th Street (now Tybrisa) was a lot more active."

Mike used to hang out with his friends on the beach.

"While there's no more half rubber on the beach, we still have some of the good old things...and we've got bocce ball now," he says. "That's a lot of fun. We have tournaments on the Fourth of July and Labor Day, and you see people on the beach that you haven't seen in years."

"I don't think it's changed that much. It still has the old flavor.

"I don't think a few condominiums are going to change things. People are going to discriminate when they come. If they don't agree with Tybee, they're gonna be gone."

Mike purchased his first cottage on Tybee for $35,000. In a small sign of the changing times, it recently sold for $150,000.

Previously, he ran Palmer & Cay Insurance Co.'s mortgage business in Savannah. He left that company in 1982 to enter the construction business, building homes in Savannah, at The Landings, and on Wilmington Island.

In 1991, he built his own home along with a duplex on Tybee and now devotes his entire operation to island development. "The market's been good to me... and it's been good to my family," he smiles.

And despite his contribution to changing its appearance, he neither wants to alter the island's basic character nor fears that his new structures will.

"I'm a businessman and I'm not ashamed of making money," he says, noting that new buildings, alone, will not alter the pleasant camaraderie which endears Tybee to both long-time residents and newcomers.

"People either love Tybee, or they hate it," he says. "It's an emotional issue. People come down, and they fall in love with it... the view of the beach... what Tybee has to offer... the privacy, the quiet... and they want to get away from the phones... to walk the beach... ride a bicycle."

Mike believes newcomers will be assimilated rather

than superimposing their big-city ways on what many feel is an island paradise.

"Obviously the island is growing, and property values have just soared the last three years," he says. "Part of that is the economy, and part is Tybee, with people discovering what they were looking for. We have a lot of people coming down from Augusta and Macon now. They're leaving on Friday afternoon and going back on Sunday night."

"And we're getting more and more local people...maybe about half now. We're getting more permanent residents."

"The weather is excellent, and September and October and April and May are our best months. It's a great

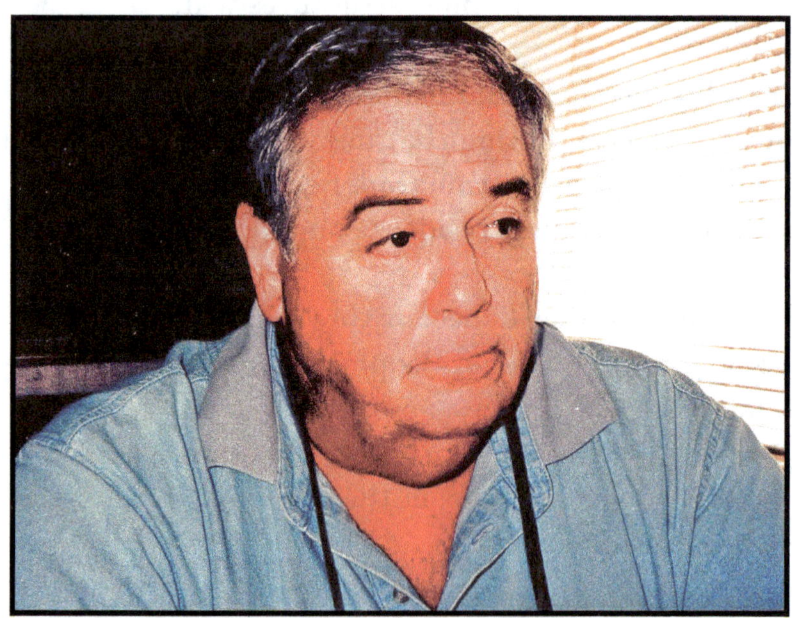

Mike discusses Tybee building boom.

place to live. It's going to become a year-round community a lot more than it has been, but the tourists are going to come in the summer like they always do to a beach community."

Mike thinks his condominiums have improved Tybee's economic base. Up front water and sewer fees for a single 14-unit condominium on which he just broke ground were $30,000.

And the condos' contribution to increases in property values - and accompanying property taxes - on the land they occupy is an asset to the island, he says, adding, "the city is reaping some of the benefits too... it's coming home."

Mike takes issue with assertions that developers are not paying enough to compensate the city for the impact their construction has on the infrastructure, which requires added sewer and water capacity, street repairs, and increased police and fire protection.

"When you pay $30,000 for water and sewer for 14 units and you increase the tax base by taking an abandoned house valued at maybe $70,000 or $80,000. and replace it with a million-dollar base, the city is benefiting," he says. "You can't solve all of Tybee's problems with that, but it's a great start...a great help."

"And," he points out, "condo residents continue to pay water and sewer bills and taxes even when they are not occupying their property."

Mike is somewhat chagrined by recent changes in rules regarding condominiums which require residential setbacks despite being located in areas zoned for business.

Those rule changes will make it difficult, if not impossible, to continue building condos in the C-l area (most of that land bordered by 14th and 18th Streets and Butler and Strand Avenues) because an insufficient amount of buildable space will be left on lots to make such structures economically viable, he says.

Since condos, in essence, are now considered residences subject to residential setbacks, some consideration was given to seeking approval to build them in residential areas "but the current political climate is basically against condominiums, and I don't fully understand why," Mike says.

"What I really don't understand is that you can build a novelty shop, a restaurant, a bar or a motel and put it right on the property line, but when it comes to a condominium it has to be 20, 10, 10, and 10 feet set back from the four property lines."

"That seems to be a little bit discriminatory to me, but that's the way it is."

Unlike some other developers, however, Mike does not seem bitter about the restrictive new rules. "It's not the end of the world," he says. "You have to adapt... but I do hope they'll ease the restrictions a little to make things better for us."

New condos are starting to line Strand Avenue.

Even if the rules are not altered, he believes competent builders will find a way to continue the island's development, perhaps by turning to duplex construction, and Mike says he has no intention of moving his business elsewhere.

"I've been tied to the island since I started building here, and this is where I will stay," he says. "I want my family to be here. Our heritage on the island is very important to me."

Mike also believes the new setback rules are not the only impediment to condo construction.

"The business district is very small, and there are few places left to develop anyway," he says, noting that most of the beach front has already been covered, and lots on side streets away from, and with little or no view of the ocean may not be desirable for condos.

About the only land left on Strand is Fannie's on the Beach restaurant and the Sundowner Motel, and the latter is already being scheduled for demolition and replacement by condos.

Mike laughs a bit uncomfortably when he discusses the current vocal opposition to condominium construction by residents who view developers as "the enemy".

Those people - who descended on city council earlier this year when it was announced that the historic DeSoto Beach Hotel would be razed for condo construction and ultimately convinced council to approve new setback restrictions and support historic preservation - blame only the builders for the loss of old island houses, he says.

"What about the people who sell us their property?" he asks. "Aren't they just as guilty? We couldn't do it if they didn't sell."

In most cases he feels builders are doing those property owners a service by giving them a profit on their investments and contributing substantially to their retirement funds.

With increasing property values, many older residents can no longer afford to live on the island, and the big profits they reap from the sale of their land makes it possible for them to live well elsewhere, he says.

The new setbacks have devalued property in the C-1

Mike Ryan stands beside one of condos he's building on Strand Ave.

District, and it will hurt property owners, according to Mike.

He says he firmly supports tax relief for older residents on fixed incomes which may make it possible for them to remain on Tybee, and he thinks those opposing condo development are not representative of most island residents.

"I think there's a silent majority that doesn't go to City Hall," he says. "They just want to live quietly and be left alone. They want to build that little shed or workshop in their yard without having to contend with all these rules."

Although he has contributed to their demise, Mike says he has an affinity for historic beach cottages and is saddened to see them disappear. He has contacted preservationists in the past, offering to donate historic old structures on property he is about to develop in an effort to have them moved to other locations and restored.

"That hasn't worked out so far, perhaps because of the cost, lack of a site on which to place them, or the condition of the houses, but it could work in the future," he says. "I don't want to just bulldoze them down. I've told the historic people I'll let them know whenever I have an old house they might be interested in and work with them on it."

He says the creation of an area - such as that around the Tybee Lighthouse - where historic houses could be moved would be a real asset for the island.

Mike believes he took a big risk when he started his first condo project.

It was after he made trips to Florida, where he examined the rapid growth of condominiums, that he decided to try his hand at such construction on Tybee's south end. "I wasn't sure Tybee was ready for condominiums, and I didn't know how it would go," he says of that decision.

He got an immediate indication when two units in Pelican Point, his first building, sold before construction was completed. That was the beginning, and "the rest is history," he says.

After selling Pelican Point, he started another and then another, each selling out while still being built. Based on Mike's impressive success, other developers joined in what has become a boom in condo construction on the south end.

"The whole face of that end of the island has changed,

and it has been very well received," he smiles. "It's been an interesting three years. "I think they have really cleaned up that end of the island. The first one I built replaced an abandoned house where drug users and everything else spent the night."

"For the most part, a condominium owner is a great neighbor. He's not there all the time, but he pays for the upkeep of his property, and he pays taxes to the city."

"We get a lot of people who buy for an investment and some who are looking to move here when they retire in five or six years."

Mike inspects condo construction.

"It's still a strong market for condos but I don't know how far it can go...that's the $64,000 question."

Condo living gives people the benefit of the ocean for less than a single-family house would cost, he says, pointing out that "the last house I sold on the oceanfront went for something like

$860,000."

"For the investor and for a second home they're more popular than houses because you've got an association that maintains the exterior and lawn, and for an out-of-town owner that is a big asset."

"You still have the use of it, and you can rent it out to help offset the expenses. Most of them that are three stories have elevators. There are a lot of pluses, and resales are great. Within four to six months, they're selling for upwards of $40,000 to $50,000 more than the purchase price."

"Where it stops, who knows?"

Even if no more condos are constructed, Mike is optimistic about the prospects for continued development on Tybee. Referring to the new $4 million restaurant under construction at the Ocean Plaza Beach Resort and the proposed new convention center on that hotel's property, he says "those ought to bring a lot more tourist business to the island, and I think there's a need for that."

"Probably in the next few years you'll see some of the old homes in the R-1 District being pulled down and replaced by duplexes, but that may take a while. The value is there, and that will open up a whole new market to people."

"I think you will eventually have to see some high-rise

hotels, but it won't be another Myrtle Beach where it's all commercial. That won't happen. But you've got a large R-1 district from City Hall to 15th Street, and it will be a long time before someone breaks that, but you just don't know."

"You've got a fairly limited area anchored by the new DeSoto units on the north and the Ocean Plaza and the condos on the south, and that's it! There's no room for expansion other than maybe hotels and motels."

"Of course, there are a few people who have the money who won't sell at any price. That's their privilege and I respect that."

"Tybee will always be Tybee. There's a certain lifestyle here. If you're coming to relax and you want the beach and you like being laid back, you're going to love Tybee Island. If you're coming for nightlife or social life, you'd better turn around and go back."

"I don't see the face or the characteristic of Tybee changing. It's anchored in."

"Tybee has a lot to offer."

POSTSCRIPT: Tourists have continued to be drawn to Tybee, just as Mike predicted, and walls of condos were built along Strand Ave. and adjacent south-end side streets. To accommodate the booming, and now year-round tourist trade, many

property owners in other areas of the island started marketing their homes for short term rentals which has resulted in a push back from opponents similar to that which followed the initial condo development.

Jenny Orr -
Tennis Star Turns Restaurateur

Her Service Becomes a Smash Hit

Jenny Orr

She's a former top athlete turned entrepreneur, and she stays as busy as Monica Seles chasing a deep backcourt lob.

Jenny Orr is a delight to watch as she scurries about in full charge of all activities at Fannie's on the Beach, her increasingly popular restaurant on the south end of Tybee.

But even during her most frenzied scamper through the Strand-side restaurant, her smile is as bright as a summer day at the shore.

Jenny looks somewhat like legendary tennis star Billie Jean King did in her heyday. She has the same attractive, short dark hair and the same delightful sparkle in her eyes.

They have something else in common as well. Jenny was also a professional tennis player and teacher.

When she was a budding teenage star, Jenny was introduced to Billie Jean, and the former tennis great gave her a still treasured tennis racquet.

Originally from Darby, Pennsylvania, Jenny moved to Savannah with her family when she was 15. Until that time her peripatetic family had lived in several areas of the U.S. and a number of foreign countries because her father, an aerospace engineer, was required to travel far afield as part of his job.

"When we got to Savannah, Mother said this is it," recalls Jenny. "She was tired of all that moving and was determined to stay in Savannah." Her mother got no real resistance, and, although her father continued his business travels, Savannah became their permanent residence.

It was a long way from her parents' birthplace in Belfast, Northern Ireland, but they quickly learned to love it. Her parents initially moved to the United States in the late 1950s when Ireland's amphibious aircraft experts, her father among them, were being heavily recruited in this country.

Her mother now spends substantial time working with Jenny in her restaurant. "Mom's always helping me around the place," says Jenny, who is delighted with both her assistance and proximity.

Jenny attended Johnson High School, then tried college for a while at Middle Tennessee and the University of Tennessee where her academic interests failed to take root.

What did root quite well was her proficiency at her sport. While still a junior, Jenny was ranked among the top 20 tennis players in the South and dropped out of college to join Washington Tennis Services as a professional player.

Later, she became a teaching professional and, at one time, was the instructor at the old Sheraton Hotel on Wilmington Island. "But the hotel was not known as a mecca for tennis, like Hilton Head," she recalls, and her career there lasted little longer than a Venus Williams drop shot.

That may have been one of her best breaks, on or off the court, since it prompted her to accept a management position with a national restaurant chain. Jenny loved the work and learned a lot about the restaurant business, which continues to serve her well as a restaurant owner.

Following a management change in her company, she was discouraged when the new guys made several operational modifications, and she began considering two job offers, one in Atlanta, the other in Jacksonville.

Seeking to gather her thoughts and decide which position to accept, Jenny headed for Tybee, since sitting beside the sea had always served as a powerful head-clearing potion for her.

Jenny recalls head-clearing visit to Tybee.

Serendipitously, she selected a spot on the south end, directly in front of what is now Fannie's. "I looked up and saw a For Sale sign on the building, and I knew at that moment that I had to have the place, no matter what it took," she laughs.

Reflecting on that time, Jenny admits it took a whole lot. She negotiated with Savannah banks for months before finally obtaining financing to purchase the building, which had housed a short-order café that closed a couple of years earlier.

That was back in 1992 when Savannah's financial institutions were less than enthusiastic about loaning money for startup businesses on Tybee.

"I finally got together with some people at SCORE (an organization composed of retired businessmen who help prospective young entrepreneurs by sharing their extensive business expertise with them). They were extremely helpful in giving me information about what companies were most interested in my kind of plans and in putting me in touch with the right people," says Jenny.

Following months of effort, she obtained the loan and was finally able to acquire the property.

"I opened it the day after I bought it," Jenny laughs.

At first her restaurant struggled along with the same sandwich-and-soft-drink fare offered by its previous owners, but Jenny had far bigger plans from the start.

After the operation became solvent, she expanded and modernized the kitchen to provide full food service and made a number of other renovations.

She also hired musicians to offer live music most weekends during the summer, enhancing Fannie's growing popularity for dining and entertainment.

But in the back of her mind from the beginning was a plan to build a second floor over the ground level building where customers could view the ocean out front. She planned to provide upscale food there and equip the new site with a posh bar.

That dream finally reached fruition this year when construction of the upper level was completed, more than doubling the restaurant's seating capacity. Her business is now flourishing, just as she imagined it would.

Jenny is currently making plans to establish a Sunday brunch upstairs and is hoping to offer live music, perhaps provided by noted Savannah bassist Ben Tucker, for her brunch customers.

Given the booming business climate on the island, she seems to have selected the right site at the right time. Jenny is delighted with Tybee's current transition, which has led local residents to become increasingly enthusiastic about and supportive of island restaurants.

"And the new Pavilion is a great addition to the south end," she says. "It is just a wonderful place and attracts a lot of tourists. It's great for business."

"Tybee is improving dramatically, particularly the business segment where owners are now making major improvements and putting a lot more money and work into their operations. Most owners are now operating their businesses themselves, unlike the old days when they were mostly absentee landlords."

Jenny believes things could be further improved by

getting more support from city officials who she feels have not moved as rapidly as island entrepreneurs in recognizing the added value local business brings to the island, but she believes there has been some recent movement in the right direction.

One of her major complaints is about the city's continuing approval of residential buildings in commercial areas.

"It just doesn't work," Jenny says. "They shouldn't be allowed in the commercial zones. People buy these expensive places and then they discover the crowds generated by adjacent businesses and the noise level from nearby music and activity."

She is particularly concerned about the recent construction of a condominium right next door to her restaurant. "I don't plan to change my operation in any way [as a result of the new building]," she says.

Condo on the left is under construction beside Jenny Orr's "Fannie's On The Beach" restaurant.

"It's just a shame that they allowed it there. I don't think those residents are going to be very happy."

But "happy" is a good description for Jenny herself.

"I love the restaurant business," she says. "It gives me a wonderful opportunity to deal with the public and to employ local residents and to help them and get to know them. I really like that. And I love Tybee, too. I can't imagine being any place else."

Her customers are delighted by her attitude and the prospect of her continued operation, which they illustrate with their repeated returns to Fannie's.

POSTSCRIPT: Jenny was right about pending problems with her new condo neighbor. Once constructed, the owner complained constantly about noise emanating from the restaurant even though the noise was there before his condo was built. Ultimately, the complainant left the island, and Fannie's has continued to thrive. A third floor has been added, providing an even more fantastic view. And those Sunday brunches were initiated and have become a popular draw, especially for those who like to savor a mimosa with their meal.

Steven Scheer - Even Hand Heads Island Court

Canine Questions Still Dog Justice

They just keep dogging him.

The dogs, that is, and their owners.

The constant requirement to rule on unleashed dogs, dogs on the beach, and barking dogs disturbing sleepless neighbors are the doggonedest problem for the judge. While he finds it distasteful, he says he must treat all these cases the same.

Municipal Court Judge Steven Scheer, a distinguished, prematurely gray-haired gentleman, looks every inch the lawyer and judge that he is. Dressed in his pinstriped lawyer's attire, he stands ramrod straight and is a well-built, tall man who is much larger than he appears when seated behind the bench in his judge's robes.

His judgements are based on both law and common sense, and most, particularly those involving juvenile offenders, are accompanied by stern lectures regarding the gravity of the offense and the liability of acquiring a criminal record.

These are perplexing cases for Judge Scheer because of his concern that succumbing to the temptation to be lenient because of the offender's age and the consequences to the individual and his family could endanger innocent parties.

This is especially true of the not uncommon occurrence of underage drinking at the beach, which he refers to as "a very disturbing problem."

Drug use on the resort island presents a similar dilemma.

But it's the dogs that are the most frequent source of consternation for both the judge and island residents.

"I really love dogs, and it bothers me to have to fine owners," says Scheer. "I learned a long time ago that everybody has a legitimate reason why their dog gets loose, but you've got to treat everybody exactly the same. If it's the mayor or a councilman, you fine them. Unless it's a very extraordinary circumstance, you've got to fine everybody."

"I hate it. Barking dog cases are the worst."

"If someone has a major offense, a DUI or something, and you have to sentence them to jail time, they'll understand that. But you fine somebody for a dog on the beach, and they can't understand it."

Although only 47, Scheer has been serving as a judge for more than 20 years, beginning as a judge pro tem in Rincon shortly after graduating from law school at the University of Georgia.

"I really liked it," he says of his initial experience sitting on the bench. "It's fun. I don't get to do much criminal work in my law practice and enjoy it. I'm involved in court fights all the time, and sometimes it's fun to have the role of referee. You certainly learn to appreciate the judge more."

"You learn something new every time you go to court, and if you can help somebody just once, you feel good about yourself."

But he got a shaky start while headed for his first jury trial as a judge when he was pulled over for speeding.

"A state trooper named James Butler stopped me, but I thought to myself, I'll fix this, and I told him I was a judge and I was on the way to a trial," recalls Scheer. "Butler didn't crack a smile. He just says: 'Law's the same for judges as it is for anybody else'."

Despite this early run in with the law, Scheer says some of his best buddies over the years have been cops and "they're the folks I enjoy having a beer with."

Early on, one of his pals told him that he had known a lot of cops who wanted to be lawyers, but Scheer was the only lawyer he had ever met who wanted to be a cop.

Incidentally, Scheer drove away from that speeding incident with a warning ticket.

Later, after ruling on a number of speeding violations as a judge, he says his offense gnawed at his conscience, and he called the police post commander to say he shouldn't have gotten away with a warning and wanted to pay his fine.

The commander declined to accept his offer, noting, somewhat wryly, that "you'll be making it up to us over time."

Ultimately, the fine would have been an easy out. Scheer has been writing wills for troopers free of charge for 22 years now!

Following his work in Rincon, Scheer became judge pro tem in Port Wentworth and Pooler, then became the regular judge for those towns. He held that position until the summer of 1991, when he was named to the same post on Tybee.

That appointment was in effect a "swap" with Herman Coolidge Jr., the previous Tybee judge, who took Scheer's judgeship in Pooler and Port Wentworth when Georgia's Judicial Qualifications Commission suggested it was inappropriate for a city to employ a lawyer and a judge from the same firm. Coolidge and Tybee's city attorney were members of the same law firm at the time.

While Scheer enjoyed his tenure at Port Wentworth and Pooler, he was delighted with the move to Tybee, and says he was particularly impressed with the Tybee police chief and the clerk of court when he arrived.

The move to the island did bring some unusual problems, however.

"One of the first cases that came before me involved a charge of sex on the beach," Scheer recalls with a laugh. "When I first heard that, I thought it was the name of a drink!"

And then there were a couple of good ol' boys from the past who seemed to forever be getting into fisticuffs with folks in Port Wentworth when Scheer was a judge there. After wearying of their frequent violations, Scheer started sentencing them to a $1,000 fine and 30 days in jail.

"That's the only way I could break them of doing it," he says.

Just before he moved to Tybee, their mother, with whom the judge became friendly over the years, called to promise him that her boys would never be in trouble in Port Wentworth again. They'd go out of town if they wanted "to do anything," she said.

Immediately after arriving on Tybee, Scheer was surprised to see the two boys in his court. The fine for disorderly conduct on Tybee at the time was $50, and one of them went directly to the clerk and paid the cash bond, while his brother continued to wait and finally was called before the judge.

"Now you know what the drill is," Scheer said he told him, "It's $1,000 and 30 days."

After court, the judge called the boy aside and noted that his brother had paid the $50 fine for the offense and wondered why he hadn't done the same.

"Cause I thought you might give me my gun back," he answered.

"It ain't gonna happen," responded Scheer, laughing at the recollection.

Aside from the plethora of underage drinking cases, Scheer says the major difference between cases on the island and those he heard in Port Wentworth is that there are no overloaded trucks on Tybee, "and in Pooler and Port Wentworth, we never had any underage drinking cases."

"That's because there was no place in those cities for them to go to drink. There was only one bar in Pooler, and I don't think any kid would want to go in there.

Judge Steven Scheer recalls some uneasy moments.

But Tybee is a resort area, and that's the biggest problem as I see it."

"Tybee's police are very good about handling underage drinking problems. The reason why they crack down on them is that several years ago there were six fatalities on the road to Tybee, and it was all kids, drinking. If you can save one kid from killing somebody else, it's worth it. Of course, you never really know that."

"You're never going to be able to stop kids from drinking though. Prohibition failed. When you try to regulate something, you just can't do it. The best you can do is stop them from drinking in public or getting behind the wheel of an automobile. We don't want a kid to get a criminal record, but if they get away with it, they're going to push it. I wish there was an answer, but I don't have it."

Judge Scheer has an impeccable reputation for being even-handed in the courtroom. "I've even fined members of my own family," he says. "They don't want to stand in front of me."

Unusually self-effacing, Scheer says he is constantly concerned about his own decisions and frequently wonders if he made the right one.

"I just hope I get it right more of the time, and that's tough," he says. "It's very easy to be pontifical, and I'm probably guilty of it more than most, but you make a mistake, and you find out about it six months later and you learn you've really affected someone's life."

Virtually all his decisions have apparently been correct, however, based on the fact that the only appeal of one of his rulings that he is aware of is presently pending.

It concerns a charge of "not obeying a lifeguard," the fine for which offense is in the area of $300 unless it is a life-threatening situation, and Scheer theorizes that the appeal is being made as a matter of principle.

He says his most difficult cases are those involving domestic violence, "because there's no 'right' answer."

In all such cases he says an immediate bond is required, "because those are the cases that scare you to death. That's where people get killed."

Another uncomfortable area for him is the occasional serious case where he must rule whether to bind the accused over to a higher court.

"I don't have any choice in these since there's such a minimal standard for probable cause," he says.

"There've been a couple of cases I heard where I said to myself 'this doesn't sound right,' but I had no choice because the probable cause standard was met, and I had to bind them over. It's not whether they're guilty or not, but simply whether the case should be heard."

The judge has had his share of unusual cases over the years.

He once had to rule on the case of a nun who ran a stop sign, and he was confronted with a real quandary involving the need to rule on whether scotch tape utilized by a stripper should be construed as sufficient apparel to avoid an indecent exposure charge.

Judge Scheer dismissed the nun's case and kidded the arresting officer by saying he was considering sending him to jail. The stripper failed to appear for the hearing, and the judge found her in contempt but says her failure to appear wasn't a major disappointment for him.

Life away from the bench can also lead to some uneasy moments for a judge.

Scheer says he was parked in his car a while back when a man approached him and asked if he was Judge Scheer.

He says the man was so big that he was looking out the window at his navel level when, with some trepidation, he admitted who he was.

"You don't remember me, but you sent me to jail," the man said.

Just when the judge's knuckles whitened, the man said he wanted to thank him for his actions. "I found religion in jail," he said. "You changed my life."

"Praise the Lord," replied Scheer, with real feeling, just before driving away.

Judge Scheer's role model is Atticus Finch, the attorney in the book and later the movie To Kill A Mocking Bird. An original poster advertising the movie was given to him by his parents when he turned 45, and it hangs in a prominent spot on a wall in his Savannah office.

"I think more lawyers of my generation go to that book or the movie (for inspiration) than anything else," he says.

Though it has occupied most of his professional life, serving as a judge is not the only governmental position Scheer has held.

He served as attorney for the Chatham County School Board during the discomfiting period when the system changed from mandatory to voluntary busing.

"We won, and I hope the community won," Scheer says. "I think the system changed dramatically for the better."

Scheer is currently chairman of the State Ethics Commission, of which he has been a member since 1991. "It's been a very interesting experience," he says of his commission service. "It makes you appreciate Chatham County a lot more."

"There are five members of the commission, and I'm the only one left from Chatham. We are very fortunate to have the quality of people we have in Chatham County."

About 90 percent of the cases the commission handles are when "people take out formal complaints about their opponents and we investigate," according to chairman. "About the only other way we're involved is when something is brought to our attention by the staff or one of the members. Then the commission can initiate an investigation."

While Scheer says a few people have used the commission as a political ploy to do harm, "for the most part people are trying to do something good for their community."

He's careful to note that the simple fact that someone is brought before the commission "doesn't mean they are guilty. Most of the time they, too, are attempting to do something good. A good many times we dismiss the charges."

The judge is adamant about having absolutely no political aspirations of his own.

A native of Savannah, Scheer has been working most of his life. At 14, he got his first job as a switchboard operator for the Jewish Educational Alliance and worked at three jobs simultaneously for most of his teen years.

Working as an electrician's helper was his most consistent employment and turned out to be the one responsible for his ultimate career.

"I was pulling wire in the attic for a sound system in Windsor Forest High School in 130-degree temperatures, and the next day I had to crawl through fiberglass insulation and duct work at Great Dane," he says.

"When you finish a job with fiberglass on you, you have to take shower with Vaseline. I said to hell with this, I'm going to college. I was the first one in the family to go."

Despite his obvious mental acuity, Scheer says he was a poor student in high school and was enrolled in a distributive cooperative education program.

"My grades were not that good except in history," he says, noting that he tested much better than his regular grades reflected, and he could never have gotten into the University of Georgia, which granted him a scholarship, based on grades alone.

Somewhat surprisingly, his grades at Georgia averaged 20 points higher than those he made at Savannah High. "That either reflects very well on Savannah High or very poorly on the university," he laughs.

One of the secrets to his improvement, he says, was attending a two-week, school-sponsored course on "How to Study."

"Until that time I had no idea how to study. Basically, the secret is to go over your notes every night and outline them. I did it and had no trouble after that."

Just after completing law school, Scheer got the then

traditional break given to new lawyers in Savannah for their first jury trial.

He was defending a man charged with a burglary at a trailer park and going up against Lionel Drew, who was then working for the district attorney's office.

"He could have killed me in that case," Scheer says of Drew, but because of the tradition, he was shown courtesy.

The jury was out only a minute before returning with an innocent verdict, after which the judge informed the jury it was Scheer's first case, and they stood and applauded.

"I thought I have arrived," he says.

That first client was on probation for burglary at the time, and Scheer smiles when he relates how justice may have ultimately triumphed.

Three weeks following the innocent verdict, the man was arrested again with a TV in his arms at the same trailer park, and during the short period between his trial and subsequent arrest, Scheer's own apartment was burglarized.

Incidentally, it was Drew, then a Recorder's Court judge, who got Scheer his initial position as a judge pro tem.

Scheer is one of four children. One of his brothers, who also has a law degree, owns a dozen T-Bones Restaurants. The other owns a restaurant in Augusta.

His sister, who was once publicity director for the famous Studio 54 in New York, has designed a line of popular and fast-selling T-shirts.

"I'm the poor boy in the family," he smiles.
One tends to write that remark off as another indication of his endearing self-deprecation when looking around his comfortable corner law office high above Drayton Street with its magnificent view of the Savannah River.

But "Po' Boy" or not, he's a pleasure to watch in action dispensing commonsense justice on Tybee.

The fact that he loves the role and the island ring clear in his pronouncements and in his plans to remain in his position "until they get tired of me."

"I really love it here," he says of Tybee. "It's the greatest place in the world. Tybee is neat. I believe the smaller the government, the better, and, like in most small towns, there is very little serious crime. The people know who the police are, and the police know who the troublemakers are."

One gets the impression that the judge would always be smiling if it weren't for those darned dogs.

***POSTSCRIPT:** Judge Steven Scheer has been honored as one of Georgia's leading lawyers while still dispensing even-handed justice as Tybee's Municipal Court Judge. Scheer now also serves as Pooler's City Attorney and heads his own law firm in Savannah.*

Leonard "Sandman" Miller - He's Building Castles in the Sand

Ephemeral Art Draws Crowds

Leonard Miller

The mystery sandcastle builder whose creations were pictured on these pages recently along with a request that readers help identify him turned out to be no mystery at all to many Tybee Island residents.

Dozens of callers identified the sand artist as Leonard Miller, a Savannah resident who frequently decorates the beach with his exotic creations.

Leonard has become known to many on the island as "The Sandman." He's a sign painter by trade and creator of sandcastles by avocation.

Leonard, with whom we talked at length after callers identified him, says he has been building castles on the beach for more than 18 years and usually constructs more than a dozen each summer, with each of them lasting as long as a week before wind and water cause them to disintegrate.

"A lot of it has to do with being in the right place at the right time," he says of his first exposure to sand sculpture. "I was in a bookstore and saw a book about sandcastle building and decided I'd try it."

He built his first castle on the south end of the beach behind the former location of Spanky's Beachside Restaurant in what is now the Econo Lodge Motel.

Leonard says he became enamored of the art form with that first rudimentary effort in the early 1980s and has been at it ever since, constantly striving to improve his now consummate skills.

Leonard Sandman Miller starts work on sand castle.

He says he learned a lot about building castle walls and turrets and other accouterments from practice and reading, but received a real education when he traveled to Canada in 1993 to enter that country's annual sand sculpture competition.

"I went to school when I went there," he says. "They do magnificent work there, and they introduced me to wonderful tools I had never considered."

"When I was exposed to the knowledge and the skills that those guys had, it was like I was starting all over. It put me on a brand-new plateau. These guys could extract details out of sand I never imagined. The knowledge I have today, much of it, comes from that visit."

Based on what he learned on that trip, Leonard now utilizes an assortment of painter's palette knives in addition to several small slivers of metal to create intricate designs on his sand art.

The Sandman has also ventured far from the beach to perform his artistry in sand. Back in 1991 he constructed a sandcastle for a show at Savannah Mall which drew high praise.

Leonard says he creates his beach art for his own enjoyment and that of the hundreds of sunbathers who invariably converge on his castles' sites to watch his work and express their admiration. "I meet a whole lot of people doing this, and I really enjoy it," he says.

The Sandman usually places a pail near his artistic endeavors to collect funds to cover the cost of his travel to the beach and the meals he consumes while working there.

Given his hefty appearance (Leonard is a mountainous man who dwarfs both his castles and the old white panel truck he drives), donations would have to be substantial just to cover the cost of his meals.

Leonard sculpts sand castle on Tybee beach.

During construction, he uses a wheelbarrow and buckets to haul water and sand to his building site, which is generally located on the beach just south of Tybee's pavilion, and just above what he estimates to be the high-tide mark, but he occasionally changes locations, moving up and down the beach.

His most recent creation was an ornate multi-towered castle featuring flying buttresses, bridges, and long curving staircases. He painted the peaks of the towers to add color to his creation. Leonard worked from early morning until late afternoon constructing the intricate design and says it normally takes about that long to build a proper sandcastle.

Even if you failed to spot him hunched over his sandy structure, you'd know he was there by the sound of his large boom box.

"I always work to music," he laughs.

Leonard says one major key to successful castles is a strong foundation, and he ensures strength in this area by tightly packing wet sand when he starts his structures.

He dedicated his current castle to Princess Diana, building it in September during the week marking the anniversary of her death. Unfortunately, that castle rapidly returned to the beach from which it came when the remnants of Hurricane Earl swept across the island two days after he erected it.

Sandman halts work to discuss project with passing couple.

Leonard plans to build another big castle to support the Muscular Dystrophy Association, dedicating it to "Jerry's Kids" in conjunction with Jerry Lewis' annual television fundraising marathon to raise funds for the MDA.

The Sandman says the quality of the sand on Tybee, along with its salt content, make ideal building materials for his artistic creations, and he can think of nowhere else he could consistently erect such castles so well.

"The beauty of this sand is its consistency," he says. "When I wet it and pack it down, it has a life expectancy of at least three or four days. Arches and bridges are a little more delicate." He plans to visit other beaches up and down the Atlantic Coast next year to participate in sand art contests from Florida to Virginia. A couple of years ago he entered such a contest at Myrtle Beach and came in second.

"I'm just glad I found this thing [sandcastle building]," he says. "It is perfect for me."

He admits, however, that 1998 has been a difficult year for his sandy art form because of the unusually intense heat.

"I've been roasting, man," he laughs.

Leonard is a native and life-long resident of Savannah, where he attended Jenkins High School. After gradu-

Crowd gathers to admire Sandman's latest creation on Tybee's south end beach.

ation, he tried a number of odd jobs before taking one assisting a sign painter, after trying to paint a few signs on his own.

That turned out to be a learning experience much like his trip to Canada.

"The painter taught me about using the proper paints and brushes for signs that made all the difference," he says, noting that until that time he had simply utilized regular outdoor house paints and brushes.

"Everyone said my design and artwork were great, but I was just using the wrong tools," he says.

Leonard also enhanced his skills by attending art classes sponsored by a church in Savannah. Devoutly re-

Leonard Miller is an imposing figure standing beside his truck on Tybee.

ligious, the side of his truck is painted with the words "Jesus Is Lord!"

"I'm glad God is in control of it," he says, eyeing ominous clouds overhead while working on his sand art.

Once completing the art course and altering his tools and material, Leonard went into business for himself and has been quite successful. His artistic signs can be found throughout Savannah and at several locations on Tybee.

The colorful sign at Fannie's on the Beach restaurant was created by Leonard, along with one just around the corner advertising a new condominium scheduled for erection by Penn Myrick.

He also painted the sign for the Waves Shop on U.S. 80 and one on a wall of the landmark T.S Chu Department Store.

Leonard says he has been coming to the beach since he was a child, and regardless of whatever success he experiences at other beaches, he intends to continue pursuing his art form on Tybee "as far into the future as I can see."

You'll find the big fellow working away at new beach creations just across from the south end parking lot every couple of weeks during the summer season.

Stop by and share his joy. Both he and his castles are a great piece of work, and the Sandman can use your contribution to assuage his hearty appetite.

Wind and tide take toll on Sandman's creation.

POSTSCRIPT: Leonard Miller became one of the best known and loved street artists in the Savannah area. A charismatic figure, he was often quoted as saying, "It doesn't cost anything to be nice." Leonard was 59 when he passed away on Jan. 5, 2016. He left a legacy of his art, hand-painted signs, and outdoor mobiles in countless places throughout Savannah and Tybee Island.

The Chu Sisters -
Preserving an Island Landmark

Beloved Store Still Going Strong

They have followed diligently, almost obediently, in the footsteps of their father, who was one of the best known and most beloved of all Tybee Island residents.

Not only have they held his businesses intact, Joan Chu Wong and Mola Chu Jung, daughters of renowned island merchant T.S. Chu, plan to continue - and perhaps even expand - into the next century.

Joan, 64, and Mola, 59, have spent their entire lives in and around the island's most famous store, T.S. Chu Co., an eclectic department store which stretches for a full block between Tybrisa Street and Izlar Avenue near Tybee's south-end beach.

Attractive and efficient, Mola handles most of the business end of the Chu enterprises, inspecting the various operations and working late into the night tallying the books.

She followed her older sister's example in manning the unique retail store's cash register when she was 7, just as Joan had done at that same age. "It was a matter of have to," says Mola. "We were poor back then. Our parents needed us. It was the way we were raised. We all worked hard."

An Atlanta newspaper article in 1947 described Mola, then 9, as a "child prodigy" who was already assisting with the store's bookkeeping. It also described her as "petite and doll-like" and responsible for "attracting visitors to the store daily."

That description still fits her well.

Joan, who manned the cash register before her sister, still handles a newer machine in the front of the store on most afternoons.

And she too, by dint of her constant smile and infectiously gregarious nature, continues to attract customers to the store. She's the kind of person you want to hug, and many visitors do just that.

Both women continue to work seven days a week, just as their father did. "But we don't work nearly as hard as our father did," says Mola. "We take off a lot more. He never took time off. He worked all the time. We work, but we still enjoy life."

For years the establishment, often referred to as "the most unusual retail store in the country," has featured dozens of departments, each containing a seemingly endless variety of merchandise.

At one time a small motel, restaurant, and beauty salon were housed on the premises, but these were shed when demands for even more merchandise mounted.

The Chu empire now includes a convenience store facing Butler Avenue just up the street; a small shopping center, including a similar convenience store and service station, liquor store, movie rental and gift shop, and sandwich and ice-cream shop on the north end of the island; numerous residential rental properties in between, and, along with the mammoth department store, a popular bar and restaurant across the street.

Sisters Mola and Joan in the office at T.S. Chu's.

Their father's nephew, P.K. "Bobby" Chu, whom he adopted after arranging for his escape from Red China 40 years ago, also owns a chain of Chu's convenience stores throughout the Savannah area.

It all began when the venerable Ting-Shan Chu, son of a successful merchant in Wenzhou, China, arrived in the United States in 1933, just out of college, as a representative of Shanghai Province at the Chicago World's Fair.

Chu accepted an invitation by his country's consul general to visit Florida following the fair and was persuaded to remain in America when the city manager of Coral Gables set him up with a gift-shop concession beside a city swimming pool, rent free.

His hard work, persistence, and penchant for saving everything he made resulted in an immediate, though small-scale, success.

Regardless of how much or how little he had, the gregarious merchant made helping others the linchpin of his life, and his generosity paid dividends from the start.

Mola handles paperwork in store's office.

When one of his Coral Gables customers, an elderly gentleman who had failed to make room reservations prior to his visit, needed a place to stay, Chu insisted that the customer take his own room. It was not until the next morning that the man realized Chu's hospitality meant his host had to spend the night in a chair on the porch.

Remembering that kindness, the man later called his benefactor, to offer him a gift shop beside the beach on Tybee when his wife became ill and they could no longer operate the business.

Chu arrived in the summer of 1933 with virtually no money, but an indomitable will to work, which lasted throughout his life.

The little 12-by-24-foot shop became the first T.S. Chu's with its proprietor working from 7 a.m. until midnight, then sleeping on the beach because he couldn't afford a regular room.

Knowing nothing about wholesaling at the time, Chu bought his merchandise retail from J.C. Penny's in Savannah, but still managed to gross $3,000 the first season, $9,000 the second, and $19,000 the third, turning all his profits back into merchandise and expansion of his shop.

After the summer months, he returned to Florida, where he continued to operate the poolside gift shop, then opened another in Burdine's Department Store in

Miami, which he operated from 5 p.m. until closing.

His diligence caught the eye of W.T. Grant, founder of the famous department store chain, who set Chu up in a Ben Franklin Five and Dime store in Florida.

Chu kept returning to Tybee in the summer, however, and ultimately opted to stay in what he referred to as his island "Utopia."

By the mid-1960s, Chu's store occupied almost an acre of space, contained 32 departments, each with more than 300 items, and he was grossing almost a million dollars a year.

While always frugal with his own lifestyle, Chu became famous for his generosity to others.

Joan and Mola recall that their home was always open to those in need and became a regular stop, particularly for Chinese immigrants, who were treated as members of their family and frequently remained for extended periods.

Chu brought his mother, Tsai Yin Chu, over from China in 1957, when she was 82 years old. It was her first departure from her homeland, and she remained with her son's family until her death in 1967.

Chu smuggled his 8-year-old nephew out of China in 1959, arranging for the boy's escape to Hong Kong from where he was flown to the United States. Chu's mother had reared Bobby when she lived in China and continued to do so once he arrived in this country.

Chu later helped bring Bobby's father and mother and two of their other children to the United States.

Bobby, now a successful entrepreneur in his own right, has inherited his adoptive father's generosity in helping others, according to Joan and Mola.

Like his Uncle Chu, he is also deeply dedicated to his family, and managed to bring his remaining three siblings to America when his business prospered.

In 1968, Chu became president of the Savannah Beach Development Co., which he was instrumental in establishing through funding from the Small Business Administration (Chu was vice consul to the SBA's U.S. Advisory Council at the time) to assist prospective Tybee businessmen in obtaining start-up capital.

Loans from the development company paved the way for expansion of a nursing home and establishment of a Ramada Inn on the island, creating hundreds of jobs at a time when few employment opportunities existed.

One of the beneficiaries of those SBA loan funds was Jim Yao, a refugee who had been a cook for a Chinese restaurant in Savannah.

Yao had no money, and Chu approached the SBA on his behalf. He was quoted as saying in broken English at the time: "He [Yao] can't speak English, on welfare, only know how to cook. Best cook in world. Chinese intelligent. If you give him a chance, he make good."

Chu's endorsement convinced the SBA to loan Yao $100,000 to establish the Dragon Palace Chinese restaurant on the site of what is now the Sunrise Restaurant on Butler Avenue.

The Dragon Palace was an immediate success and remained so until it was destroyed by fire. The Sunrise remains in the Yao family and Jim's son, Paul, has opened several other restaurants in Savannah.

Of his work with the development company, Chu was quoted in an Atlanta magazine years ago as saying: "Government money help Savannah Beach (the city's name before it reverted back to the name 'Tybee' in the 1960s) get going. Make Savannah Beach successful. No merchant go bankrupt here. Money paid back with interest. If you lazy, just take money and spend it. That's no good. Got to work hard and pay back. But got to have something to start."

It was not only recent foreign arrivals that Chu assisted. He became the guardian of Tybee entrepreneur and former councilman Phil O'Dell when he was a child, contributing substantially to his upbringing and future success.

Phil remembers accompanying Chu on frequent trips throughout the area as a young man. "He was always interested in anything new and had a special interest in fast-food operations," says Phil, who developed his own interest in such operations on those early trips with his guardian.

Joan mans cash register beside T.S. Chu's entrance.

Phil, who worked with various Chu enterprises as a young man, later owned and operated the Arby's Roast Beef franchise at the island's south end and is currently completing work on a new fast-food restaurant expected to open this month on the north end.

Chu invariably found a spot in one of his enterprises to employ islanders who were down on their luck. Forty beach residents, comprising two percent of Tybee's entire permanent population at the time, were employed by Chu in the mid-1960s.

A quintessential optimist, Chu was always active in community improvement and, appropriately, was elected president and life member of the Optimist Club in the 1950s.

Described as a one-man chamber of commerce, it was Chu who proved instrumental in persuading Cecil Day, an Atlanta developer and father of state Rep. Burke

Day, to build his first Days Inn on Tybee.

Often referred to as "Mr. Savannah Beach," word of Chu's entrepreneurial acumen spread throughout the eastern United States.

Dwight D. Eisenhower made it a point to stop at Chu's store when he visited the island prior to being elected president. The then Gen. Eisenhower asked for a fishing cork which was not in stock, and Chu had it waiting for him the following day, fulfilling the promise he made when starting the store that if a customer wanted any item, he would supply it, and establishing the "Chu's has everything" reputation.

Joan laughs when she recalls her father's embarrassment when he was told that Eisenhower had called his store "a great institution."

"Dad thought he meant it was some sort of mental institution until I explained it to him," she says. "Then he was delighted."

Throughout most of his career, Chu was ably assisted by his wife (the former Mae Jung of Savannah whom he married in 1937) and daughters.

Mola and Joan worked in their father's store after school and during the summer until they left for college.

Joan graduated from Mount St. Agnes in Baltimore

and Mola from Immaculata in Philadelphia. Both returned to Tybee after graduating and became full-time employees at their father's department store.

"But it wasn't all work," says Mola. "We loved the beach, and we had lots of time to play on it with our friends, and the old bowling alley by the pier was always fun. Dad was pretty easygoing with us. It was Mother who was the strict one."

Both sisters married in their 20s. Joan has three children, and Mola has two.

Joan took a brief break from store operations when she and her former husband purchased the Sundowner Motel, but she soon returned to the family operation.

Chu kept his family close by offering each member not only unreserved love but an opportunity to succeed financially.

"In building a family you must first build education, then good will," he said. "Must be kind to people, and you got to provide a decent living for your educated people for them to stay in a small town."

"If I want my children to stay near me, I have to provide opportunities for them, otherwise they move away to jobs. They sacrifice one or two years, but no one going to sacrifice for a lifetime if they don't have to. Small towns most important. Need good people to build them."

It wasn't simply the financial assistance that kept his children in the family business, however.

"We respected him and never wanted to do anything to disappoint him, and it's a tradition among Chinese for families to stay together," Mola says.

Joan and Mola say they tried to get their father to retire several years prior to his death in 1984, "but he couldn't stand it. He just got nervous."

During his last years, while turning the day-to-day business operations over to his daughters, Chu continued to roam the store, checking its endless inventory, and chatting cheerily with customers.

Knowing his operation was in good hands, he was also able to spend time with his five grandchildren, "who he just worshiped," says Joan.

Mola smiles while recalling early days in store.

"We had to buy a new stroller every month because he would take the grandchildren down to the beach and push the strollers into the water with them," she says.

She recalls the time her father took the children to Morrison's Cafeteria in Savannah when they were still tots and had to solicit the help of friends in the restaurant to assist each grandchild through the serving line.

"And when they were in the seventh and eighth grades, he taught them all how to drive," she says. "He would take them down to Fort Screven on weekends when no one was around, and he'd get out and let them drive around by themselves."

Both Joan and Mola say their father helped hundreds of people while keeping his generosity a secret.

Joan recalls that at his funeral, which was attended by hundreds, a stranger walked up to praise her father's generosity, disclosing that years earlier Chu had provided him with money when he told him he was broke and about to lose his house.

Both sisters say their father constantly tried to give something back to the country he felt had given him so much.

"I remember how he smiled when he received his first Social Security check," says Mola. "He was so proud."

Then she disclosed that her father gave the money from every one of his Social Security payments to people in need.

Mola's children, Teresa and Monica, now in their 30's,

are continuing the Chu dynasty by operating stores in the family's north-end shopping center and are planning further acquisitions.

And Mola and Joan are currently contemplating conversion of the landmark department store, which they say is now "a little bit out of style," into a shopping mall. Mola says she is also considering other development plans on the island but is not ready to discuss these at the present time.

One thing is certain, the Chu name will always remain indelibly intertwined with Tybee and the entire Savannah area.

It's a family tradition.

POSTSCRIPT: Joan Chu Wong passed away June 28, 2006, at age 71. Mola still remains active in the operation of Chu enterprises and T.S. Chu's, now approaching its 90th year, continues to operate as a department store, just like its founder intended.

Lance Smith - Islander Enjoys Living Like a Millionaire

Lawyer Succeeds at Everything Except Matrimony

You've seen him on the phone book.

You've seen him on billboards.

You may even have seen him in court, and if you've spent any time sampling Tybee's night life, you've seen him socializing, usually in the company of an attractive woman while attracting a coterie of confidants.

He's bigger than life!

He's Lance Smith who now appears, sans his most recent former wife, on the back cover of the Savannah telephone book.

But he claims that all he yearns for is a quiet, contemplative life at the beach.

Lance reveals his aspirations and some of his exploits while leaning back against a railing on the deck of his sumptuous beachfront home on Tybee's north end.

During much of the conversation he's joined by a breathtaking brunette who sprawls distractingly on a nearby lounge chair while glancing up at Lance occasionally to suggest that he curtail certain titillating topics.

The dune side deck looks directly over the ocean and beach, a view featuring frequent strolls by sometimes sensuous, scantily clad beach bunnies which Lance admits...during one of his friend's brief absences to fetch us drinks...he is not averse to perusing.

"I'm not into bar-hopping or girl-chasing," he declares, while indulging in such a perusal. "I do like beautiful women. I simply admire beauty."

The view from his previous residence, a cottage adjacent the municipal parking lot and business district on Tybee's south end, was similarly spectacular. That house too was on the oceanfront "but it was a lot more congested there during the summer," he says, noting that he had no intention of moving, but when he was shown his current property just outside the pillars leading into Ft. Screven, "I had to have it."

It's a rambling, elevator-equipped, three-story structure which draws droves of Lance's friends and wannabe buddies every weekend. There were more than a dozen men, women, boys, and girls frolicking about the place when we got together on Saturday afternoon.

One of the male visitors ventured out a bit unsteadily to interrupt our conversation saying, "I just want to tell you that this is one of the finest individuals I have known in all my years as a top attorney in Washington." "This is him, right here," he drawled, patting Lance on the shoulder to emphasize his point.

Lance, a loquacious interlocutor, looks more like a middleweight boxer than the successful lawyer and real estate developer he is.

Clients, accustomed to seeing him clad in expensive suits and monogramed dress shirts at his law offices beside his big billboard on Abercorn Street in Savannah, might not recognize him in his beach mode. Like most on Tybee, he dresses in beach-bum casual, wearing his loafers sockless and donning shorts and a T-shirt for most island outings.

Lance is a native Savannahian whose father, a merchant mariner, was lost at sea when his ship was sunk by a German sub off Nova Scotia during World War II. He spent much of his youth at the beach, coming out each summer before finally making it his permanent address in the early 1990s.

Now 58, Lance has pretty much been there and done that and returned for a second or third round.

That's certainly true of marriages. He's had three, although the second sort of didn't count since it was more like a 30-day fling, he says, noting: "My lawyer on that one said he'd never seen anyone pay so much for so little."

Each of the other two lasted 18 years.

"I've been married my entire life," he smiles, noting that his first trip to the altar came at age 19 and "I really like companionship."

Although he doesn't discount the possibility of making yet another trip down the well-worn aisle, Lance says his most recent divorce put a big dent in his economic situation.

"You have so much you have to get back together, you know?" he explains. "You have to regroup. That's what I've been doing for the last year: regrouping. That takes a lot of effort, and time."

Regrouping won't include acquisition of another yacht like the one he once lived aboard, however, since "that divorce took care of all my sailing and boating."

Lance says his son by his first marriage, now a screen-writer in Hollywood, recently filmed a movie entitled "Love Shack" at his beach house but wouldn't even offer him a walk on part in the film.

He laughs when recalling that he gave cursory consideration to erecting a sign outside his house adorned with the movie's title but ultimately thought better of it.

After a successful career in real estate, law and politics, Lance retired in 1980 and sailed to Key West, where he lived on his 50-foot ketch while enjoying a laid-back, hedonistic lifestyle.

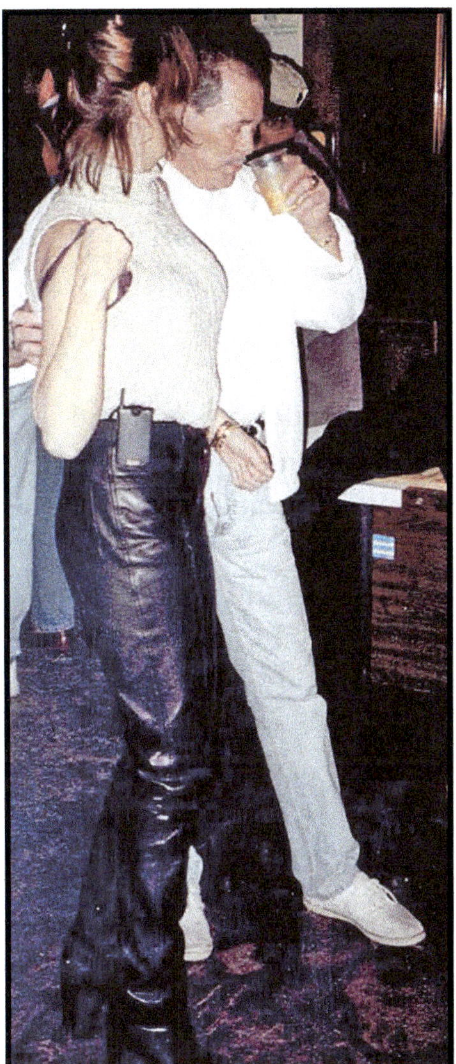
Lance Smith steps out with one of his friends.

"We'd wake up in the morning and go to breakfast and stay there until about 11 a.m., then come back and have a nap. Then we'd work around the boat for three or four hours. Then cocktail hour would start, and the cycle would begin again. It was kind of like Tybee."

After a Key West bar that Lance owned a piece of went bust, he says he hauled all the bar's booze back to his ketch and "my boat became the cocktail place.

I liked Key West a lot."

It was the IRS that eventually forced him back to work. "They crippled me," he says.

Kissing his Key West retirement goodbye, he returned to rekindle his legal profession in Savannah, and between that and developing real estate on Tybee he's been at it ever since.

Lance now has a large share of the accident-claims business in the area with his firm handling about 500 cases a year "but the real money I've made has always been in real estate," he says.

He developed the Tybee Lights condominiums and recalls paying only $19,000 for the south-end beach house on which he has a current contract for $250,000.

"I don't know where else you can go and get that kind of return on your money," he says. "I've owned a good bit of real estate on Tybee, and it's always been a real money maker for me."

Aside from matrimony, Lance has been successful at most of his ventures. He earned both his undergraduate and law degrees from the University of Georgia, passing his bar exam before he graduated.

"I was the only lawyer in my law class," he smiles.

He was also Georgia's youngest elected state representative, taking office after winning the Chatham County seat when he was just 26. "I was actually elected before I was old enough to take the oath of office," he recalls, noting that his birthday occurred just in time for him to be sworn in.

Lance served in the statehouse for four years before losing interest and stepping down. "It just got to be the same thing all the time," he recalls. "The same people, the same problems."

It wasn't long before he returned to public service, however.

Lance was Tybee's city attorney and municipal judge for about ten years at different times "depending on who was in office," he says. "I had a tearaway robe, like a football player's uniform, I was in and out so often."

He was motivated to return to public service by an incident which occurred in front of his south-end cottage.

"I looked out there, and they were digging up the dunes, hauling the sand up to the beach at the north end," he recalls. "They were literally destroying the beach, and they were letting people come out and dig up all the sea oats in front of my house. I went out there one day and the oats were all gone."

Lance confronted the workmen and called city officials, but no one paid any attention to his complaints, so he took matters into his own hands, parking his Buick in the middle of the earth ramp used to bring equipment to and from the beach to dig and haul the sand.

"I locked it and left it there," he says. "They couldn't get their bulldozers onto the beach or their trucks off it." The mayor wasn't happy, but the work was stopped.

Lance later took the city to court, stopped the work permanently, then joined the opposition forces in the next Tybee election to get rid of the mayor. That's how he wound up being appointed to the positions of city attorney and judge.

Lance enjoys drink, dance and conversation all at once.

Later, the ousted mayor and Lance reconciled, and Lance supported him in a later election, helping him to recapture the office.

But that's all past history for him now.

Lance says he hasn't been to City Hall for some time after "I told them to leave me alone and I'd leave them alone." He says he used to feel he had alienated some people, but he's no longer concerned that folks might not like him.

"I asked a friend awhile back what was wrong with me," he says, and the friend replied "Lance, why should anybody like you? You live on an island; you drive a Rolls Royce, and you've got a good-looking wife. Why should they like you?"

"That explains it," laughed Lance. "I can accept that. Why should they?"

But he admits, when asked how he'd like to be thought of, that he wants to be remembered as "not as bad as people think," and he plans to remain in the spotlight for a while, right there on the back of your telephone book.

He acquired that coveted spot with a 30-second decision four years ago. "A salesman came out when it became open to ask me if I wanted it," he says. "He said I had 30 seconds to decide, after which it would be gone. Then he said I had 20 seconds, then 15, then ten.

"Then he said 'You've got just three seconds now. You want it or not?'

"I said I'll take it." Lance said he was familiar with marketing and figured if you were going to advertise you'd best do it big.

Besides, he feels his advertising budget, which tops out at $100,000 a year, is small compared with large firms, with the tenth largest firm in the country spending $6.5 million a year on advertising.

That phonebook picture had to be changed recently because it included both Lance and his latest former wife.

"They didn't give me a rebate when I dropped her out of the picture," he grins.

Looking toward Tybee's future, he expects things will change as real estate grows more expensive.

"I'm not a condo lover although I build condos," he says. "I hate to see the old beach houses go, but they will someday. They have to."

He also thinks the island's 35-foot height restriction will someday be dropped.

"When I was city attorney, I was told that the reason you couldn't go any higher was because we didn't have a fire truck with a ladder on it big enough to reach over 33 feet," he says.

"I always thought that was the reason [for the height restriction], but apparently there's more reasons than that."

Even the present height limit blocks views of the ocean, and "I've got a philosophy about that," he says.

"If you want an ocean view, buy oceanfront property. Don't buy two lots back and then complain when somebody builds something in front of you, and if a developer wants to build a high rise let him and let him buy a fire truck big enough to handle a blaze at the place."

Lance says he no longer harbors any political aspirations or professional goals.

"I just want to be right here," he says, glancing contentedly around the house and deck and out to the ocean beyond.

"I like my situation. I wish I didn't have to leave the island even now."

"I want to live like a millionaire. I don't want to die like one."

POSTSCRIPT: Lance passed away not long after this story was published. His son, Lance Smith Jr., the successful screenwriter and novelist to whom

he refers, who had been living in Hawaii, moved to Savannah in 2018 to be nearer to surviving relatives. He passed away in 2020 at age 59, while under hospice care after suffering from early-onset Alzheimer's Disease.

Burke Day -
State Rep. Optimistic About Island's Future

Son of Days Inn Founder Continues Family Tradition

Burke Day

Burke follows his father's footsteps. And his own sons are following in his.

It's a tradition in this family. "Family" isn't tokenism for them. It's their foundation.

"It sort of brings things full circle," says Burke, watching his three sons shoot hoops in a net beside their home on Tybee, pride pervading his voice and eyes.

Burke's writing a book about the current generation and its future prospects entitled "Leadership for Grabs." He has an optimistic outlook.

Burke sees a bright future for today's youngsters, despite their concern about diminishing chances for economic success. The key will be a return to traditional family values and the extended family unit of our grandparents and great-grandparents, he says.

Burke seems optimistic about most things.

He's Rep. Cecil Burke Day Jr., serving his second term as the representative of District 153, which covers the island areas of Chatham County. He claims to be a politician by happenstance rather than predilection.

He's written other books, the most successful being "Day by Day," the story of his father's "simple formula for business success."

That book has sold exceedingly well, particularly overseas where it has sold in 137 countries. His father was Cecil Burke Day, Sr., the founder of the Days Inn motel chain.

The first motel in that chain was built on Tybee. It still stands, recently refurbished, on Butler Ave.

His father, then in his mid-30s, had retired after a successful career in Atlanta real estate at the time he built the motel in 1970.

He consulted his family before initiating the enterprise. They voted on the proposal, and it carried, four to two, with Cecil's wife and son, Clinton, former state senator representing Fulton and Gwinnett Counties ("Clint's the real politician in the family," according to Burke), casting the dissenting votes.

Bringing the family into the decision was a major reason for the motel's success, Burke feels. "It made us a part of it. We were all dedicated to making it a success."

His grandmother, mother, sister, and all his brothers worked at the motel when it opened. "I was one of the first ditch diggers and one of the first maids," recalls Burke.

He emulated his father when he sought his first elected position as a councilman on the island, discussing his plan with his family. They endorsed the proposal enthusiastically.

"They were my legs," says Burke of his wife, Sally, and three sons. In his twenties Burke contracted an extremely rare degenerative muscle ailment which causes muscle loss rather than gain from extended exercise. He says only he and one other person have been diagnosed with the ailment, which is termed "Day's Syndrome."

To prevent further deterioration, he moves about Georgia's state house in a mechanized wheelchair and uses a cane to navigate short distances. "The hardest thing I've had to learn is to accept help from other people," he says.

But Burke is optimistic about a remedy for his ailment as well. Following extensive tests and experiments on him, researchers are very close to pinpointing the exact location of the genetic marker, he says. "And they already know which gene is defective and what to do to fix it when they find it."

His sons distributed cards urging Tybee residents to support their father's race for council when they went door to door trick or treating on Halloween.

Burke followed his father's example in entrepreneurship as well. As a youth on the island he earned his spending money working at Chu's Department Store and other area businesses.

And he concocted a drink by blending a variety Kool-Aid mixes together into what he called "Weirdo," peddling it on the beach behind a group of beach youths who sold peanuts to sunbathers. His father had sold soft drinks from a streetside stand in his yard when he was a boy.

Originally from Savannah and the son of the Rev. Lon Day, former pastor of the old Emmanuel Baptist Church on Bull Street, his father was devoutly religious. He listened "to that inner voice" when he formulated plans to build his first motel, says Burke of his father.

During his ownership of the chain, a Bible was placed in each room, and guests were encouraged to take it with them when they departed. He also arranged for a minister to be available to all guests who sought religious consultation and had a rule that no alcohol was distributed at any of his motels.

Cecil Day Sr. was initially inspired to enter the motel business during a cross-country family trip, according to Burke. He was appalled by the high prices of the standard motel chains and "moaned and groaned about them the entire trip," says Burke.

He felt that decent, inexpensive lodging should be available for travelers with limited funds and believed this family market was virtually untapped. "His experience on that trip started the idea," says Burke.

But he also admits that earlier exposure to his mother's habit of renting out cots on the porch of her house on Tybee's south end may have contributed to the hostelry idea's germination.

His father's goal, once the initial motel proved successful, was to have a chain of 300 within ten years. "He truly felt that this was his ministry," says Burke.

Day reached that goal in just eight years. The chain was among the top ten in the country by the time of his death at age 44.

Burke, himself, seeks spiritual guidance in most of his endeavors. He says he "looked to the heavens" when he moved to Tybee permanently in the late 1980s after his own successful real estate ventures in the Atlanta area. He became involved in real estate development on the island and surrounding areas but was wondering about other meaningful activities to pursue.

"There was a Divine Hand involved in my getting into politics," he says. "People kept asking me to run for council, and after a while I figured that might be the message."

At that time he says he shared the relatively low opinion many have of politicians, but he figured he should follow the suggestions in case they really were the message he had sought.

"When I learned I had won that first election, I said I thought they ought to have a recount," he laughs.

But once immersed in the cauldron of Tybee politics, he was attracted to the island's microcosmic democracy. While it was not all Georgia peaches and cream (Burke was involved in a couple of political controversies, including one heated difference of opinion with Mayor Walter Parker), he says he learned a lot about island operations and "how it feels to be out there on the line" in front of neighbors and

Rep. Burke Day.

constituents.

"It's a hot seat is what it is, and it should be," he says. Burke says he and Pat Locklear were the boat rockers in that first term on council "but I believe if the boat can't survive the rocking, it might not should be in the water."

He sought and won a second term, then resigned to seek his current seat in state government which had been vacated when Eric Johnson resigned to run for the senate.

Burke says the lessons he learned as a Tybee councilman have served him well. "Nobody can go toe to toe with me in Atlanta after the Tybee experience, and I'm very proud of that."

One thing he says he learned both on council and at the statehouse is that politicians are not really scoundrels. "They're motivated to do the right thing, even when I don't agree with them," he says.

"The politicians in Atlanta are some of the nicest folks you'd ever want to meet. When you put your name on the line, you try to do your best."

And he's learned the hard truth that politicians are not forgiven for their mistakes, "they're remembered for them. In the private sector you can make a mistake, and you're applauded for it. People say you were trying."

Burke says he's particularly impressed with the way Tybee's government can stretch its economic resources to provide services to the island's residents.

"They get blood out of a penny," he says. "I was utterly amazed. I don't think you'll see much better management of taxpayer money than what you see on a local level."

And he thinks involved citizens such as those on Tybee would be the salvation of government in general. "If they could get 90 percent participation by the voters in other elections like they do on Tybee, the problems we see in government today could all be eliminated within four years," he says.

Burke has a particular affection for Tybee as "the heart of American business.

"You can find a plumber and a millionaire sitting side by side, shoulder to shoulder, at a coffee shop, cursing the very government they helped to form only two years earlier. It's a very unpretentious place. The rule is 'be thyself.' My Dad loved to come down here and go by the Tybee Market where Mr. Hosti treated him like any other customer, not like some V.I.P."

The increasing burden of property taxes on citizens is one of his major concerns. Pushing for legislation for more equitable evaluation of property is high on his current list of priorities since he feels inflated evaluations cause many property owners to pay for value that's not present.

One of his answers for covering the revenue loss resulting from reduced evaluations is to permit higher taxes on hotels and motels. With tourism growing daily he thinks it makes sense to tap into this market to generate revenue.

To those who oppose this premise, Burke says "if the value is there, the tourists will come and pay for it." Besides, if other revenue sources are not tapped, government will invariably turn to increased residential property taxes as the answer "and there's no quicker way to create a ghost town," he warns.

Given his background in the real estate and motel business, Burke is intellectually prepared to deal with arguments from hotel owners. Of his own "unchosen" profession, he feels that elected officials should get back to the basics.

"The mission of government is to steer the boat, not row the boat," he says. "The mission of the private sector is to make a profit, and the mission of the volunteer sector is to pick up the slack between the two. Whenever those three are left alone, they do fine but whenever one crosses the line, things get fuzzy like they are today."

Burke uses an analogy about driving over the Talmadge Bridge from Savannah to Hutchinson Island as an example. "How fast would you drive across that bridge if there were no regulations, no speed limit?" he asks, then follows up with: "How fast would you drive if there were no guard rails?"

Government, he believes, should serve as a guard rail for the citizenry.

And local government will become ever more important with the trend toward downloading former federal programs to states and municipalities, he says.

Burke's family has been tied to Tybee for several generations. His grandparents, who lived in Savannah, came out frequently. They first met on the old train to the island. Later, they introduced his father to the beach.

"And Dad brought us (Burke, his three brothers, and a sister) down every summer." The seven of them stayed in a little two-bedroom cottage at the corner of 11th Street and Butler Ave. which his father had purchased for $15,000 ("nothing down, and paid off a little at a time," says Burke).

"Dad never even allowed a telephone in the place, and our only TV had a broken antenna." That little cottage, located just behind the Day family's spacious current residence, still remains in the Day's property portfolio.

Burke recalls that his father would never permit his children to go down to 16th Street on weekends because of the boisterous activities there. "And every year he'd make all the boys get short crew cuts. You could always tell who we were out in the water because of our glistening heads."

"We thought it was barbaric. We wondered why he'd make us live like that."

The answer came with later reflection, particularly when Burke was working on the book about his father and learning to look at him from a writer's, rather than a son's, perspective. Burke says he believes the strict rules stemmed from lessons his father learned in boot camp about "forging a unit together" when he joined the Marine Corps.

He wanted his children to learn to rely on one another, to be a team, says Burke, And it worked. "When we Day boys were picked on, we'd stick together," Burke smiles. "To this day, my brothers and our sister are very close."

Burke says he's trying to instill the same sense of family and teamwork in his sons. "That's one of the reasons I brought my family to Tybee," he says.

Even before they moved their principal residence to the island, they, like his father's family before him, came to the island every summer. Burke wanted his children to get to know some of the people he knew when he was their age.

"It helps you to know where you come from," he says. "Family is an important thing. They're the fourth generation of Days who have lived here. It's a very humbling feeling.

"And I wanted the boys to get to know each other. To work together. To learn to enjoy some of the simple things, like flying a kite. To use their imagination. Those are things that last a lifetime."

While he has forgone the requirement for crewcuts among his boys, interestingly, they've opted for those short haircuts on their own.

Talk about coming full circle! "They actually wanted burr cuts," says Burke. "I couldn't believe it."

Another standard value in the Day family, according to Burke, is that when a kid becomes 18, he's expected to be on his own, "to row his own boat."

He says that will apply to his own boys as well. The oldest is now 16, so it won't be long now. He was out getting driving practice with his mother while his father chatted about family values.

Burke became immersed in memories of his childhood days at the beach on a recent tour of his old stomping grounds. We drove by the little cottage on 11th Street and passed the Breakfast Club where an ice cream parlor once stood. Burke used to dip ice cream there as a boy.

Then we went by Chu's, where he worked in the hardware area, and continued down to 18th street, where his grandmother sublet a house after her husband died. "She didn't have a lot of money after the reverend died and would rent out cots on the porch," Burke recalls.

Burke later purchased and subdivided property at the corner of Strand and 18th. "I never dreamed back then I'd ever be doing anything like that," he says.

And he was instrumental in getting those palm trees lining the parking lots along the beach, having headed a group which raised funds for the project.

Burke and his father once camped out in an old station wagon in the parking lot beside which the palms now stand. His father covered the car's windows with maps acquired free in those days from gas stations. "I felt like I was inside a body looking around at those maps on the windows with the light coming through from the street lights," he says. "The blue lines on the maps looked like blood veins."

Before the family bought their cottage they also occasionally stayed at Cobb's Apartments, just across the street from the parking lot.

One of his fondest memories is of hitchhiking to the island from Atlanta with his father. Burke was only four at the time. "We had no trouble getting rides down," says Burke, who also recalls that his father always picked up hitchhikers when he was driving, especially men in uniform.

Burke concluded his trip down memory lane by pulling into the parking lot of the original Days Inn.

"He never put an apostrophe in the 'Days.' From the git-go he said, I never want to be owned by the stuff on the sign."

While chatting in the parking lot there, the new owner recognized the founder's son and insisted on having him inspect one of the refurbished rooms.

It had been 16 years since Burke had been inside a room at the old motel. He beamed as he inspected the fresh paint and furnishings, seeming as proud as the new owner was of the improvements.

"You know you can sell a man a car, but you can't drive it for him," Burke observed. It was obvious that he approved of the new owner's ability at the wheel.

In his new book, which he expects to be published next year, Burke says he will reassure youngsters that times will not be as dismal as some suspect.

"They and their wives are not going to have to work two jobs just to live in a big old house," he says.

"They'll make history by redefining American values, asking questions like 'what is really important'."

But he believes Medicare will be a failed system.

"It won't be taking care of me," he says. Then, motioning toward his sons, he adds: "I'll probably die in one of those guys' houses."

"People are going to get back to old family values, the extended family where people take care of their own."

As to his own future, Burke has no firm plans. "Sometimes I think I'm God's Gypsy," he says. "The only thing I've ever wanted to do is what my maker wanted me to do."

He does expect to seek reelection as a representative, but beyond that and completing the "Leadership for Grabs" book and a historical novel in the James Michener mode that he's been working on for eight years, Burke just doesn't know.

"I'll take it as it comes," he says.

And, of course, he'll be looking up for further advice.

POSTSCRIPT: Cecil Burke Day Jr. retired from public office in 2011 after serving eight consecutive terms, 16 years, in the Georgia House of Representatives. While there he was instrumental in getting the Stephens-Day Bill passed to ease the burden of home owners' property taxes. Tybee's new Burke Day Public Safety Building, which

serves as both City Council chambers and police headquarters, was dedicated in his honor in 2015. Burke passed away at his island home on March 5, 2017. He was 62.

Sylvia Gott - Nonagenarian Lady's Still "Gott" Rhythm

She Loves That Late Night Music

Find music and you'll find Sylvia, but only in the evening.

She sleeps until well after noon each day. It's not because she's lazy, nor is it attributable to the fact that she turned 90 this year.

Sylvia Gott, an energetic, gregarious lady whose appearance and stamina belie her age by decades, has hardly lost a step over the years.

Always meticulously coifed and resplendent in fashionable attire despite Tybee's heat and humidity, she still drives a car days and cuts a wicked rug nights on island dance floors.

"My problem is that I can't get to sleep until I see the sun coming up," she smiles, when questioned about her late-rising habit. "I've been a night person my entire life."

Habitues of island nightlife quickly confirm that statement. Sylvia routinely bops about Tybee bistros, lingering until they close before heading home around 3 a.m. While she stops by most of the south-end night spots, Doc's Bar is her favorite hangout.

"It's the music I go out for," she says. "I just love the music, and I've always loved to dance; I don't drink much," although she does admit to sipping a couple of vodka cocktails each evening.

Sylvia is out on the town five nights a week, Wednesday through Sunday, savoring the summer's music and good times. Asked what she does on Monday and Tuesday nights, when most bandstands are dark, she chuckles, "I rest up for the remainder of the week."

Since arriving on Tybee a year ago, Sylvia has become a familiar fixture at Doc's, where she holds court regally at a table at the front window adjacent to the bar's band stand.

Admirers gather around her table for conversation, an occasional dance, and to enjoy her precise playing of maracas and tambourine in accompaniment to house musician Charlie Sherrill.

"I love to listen to Charlie," she says. "He's such a great musician. He's really too good for here."

Her admiration is reciprocated.

Sylvia sits in front of Doc's Bar.

"She's just great," says Charlie. "She helps me keep the rhythm when I get a little off. Sometimes I look over at her when she waves her maracas over her head, and I just say 'Wow.' She's good."

Sylvia laughs regarding her solo rhythm section performance, observing, "I don't even get musician's scale for my work."

She's more than a little knowledgeable about musicians' pay. Sylvia has performed for more than 80 years, starting as a pianist at the age of 6. She took to the trumpet in her teens, playing both classical and dance music as she and the century gyrated through their Roaring 20s to the tune of the "Charleston" and the squeak of the speakeasy's swinging doors.

Sylvia escaped the dry days of Prohibition during her residence in Toronto, Canada, where liquid libations remained legal.

Ultimately, she switched to the drums. "They were a lot easier on my lips than the trumpet," she smiles.

Hers has been a rollicking good life filled with music she was born to play, her family tree having been decorated with a host of talented musicians.

Her father, H.D. Worth, was the Stuart, Florida, Concert Band director whose band Sylvia played trumpet with at age 12. Her brother played keyboard, sax, accordion, and drums; her mother, the baritone sax in her husband's band; and an aunt excelled on the French horn.

"There was always music in the family," she says. "We used to play together at family gatherings. We had our own band."

Sylvia was born in the village of Patchogue on Long Island, New York, where her father, who initially worked in the harness business and as a charter fishing boat captain, started performing with orchestras in New York just after the turn of the century.

When she turned 9, the family headed toward southern sunshine when her father took the band director's job in Florida. She continued performing in his band throughout her school years in Stuart, a town she says she adored and in which she knew most of the people.

"But everything there has changed now," she laments. "At my age, I've outlived all of 'em."

At 19, she married her first husband, George, who she says she met "on a dance floor in Stuart." After the wedding, George's career as an insurance agent took them to Cleveland, Ohio, Syracuse, New York, and Toronto, Canada. Sylvia sat in with bands in those cities during their 17-year marriage, taking time out to give birth to two daughters, Dale and Patricia.

Patricia, now Pat Whitney, has operated Poor Pat's restaurant on Tybee for the last 20 years.

Not long after her divorce, Sylvia was reunited with a man who was her teenage heart throb.

Rodney, a traveling musician, was playing trumpet at a dog track in Miami, where her father had come full circle in his career by returning to the harness-making business at the Hialeah Race Track.

"I looked over and saw him playing in the band and told my father I thought it was Rodney, who I had a crush on when I was 15," she smiles. "I hadn't seen him since he left Stuart to move up to Boston more than 20 years earlier."

"We sent him a note, and he remembered us and came over. He was so glad to see us."

After a brief courtship, the two were married and spent the next 41 years, until his death in 1966, playing together in bands.

Sylvia says Rodney had previously performed with several big-name bands and often wrote arrangements for the groups. "He was a very fine musician," she smiles.

They had two boys, Gary and Rodney, both of whom volunteered for service in the Vietnam War. "Gary, who was in the Army, did more than his share over there," says Sylvia.

Rodney, a decorated hero, was killed in the war. He

was an Air Force sergeant who "was working as a radio intercept operator" when, at 21, he reportedly died when his plane went down over Laos, she says.

"They didn't tell me what happened or exactly what he did," she says. "They didn't find his plane for eight months, and when they did, they judged that he was dead. That's all I know. They said I might read about it in the history books some day, but I don't expect I'll live that long."

Whatever it was, he must have exhibited extraordinary heroism. The Air Force named a barracks for him at a base in Japan. A theater in Taiwan and a dining hall at Kelly Air Force Base in San Antonio, Texas, were also named in honor of Rodney H. Gott.

Sylvia attended the dedication at Kelly AFB. "I was escorted to the ceremony on the arm of a general," she says proudly. "They had an armed honor guard and a complete, beautiful ceremony for him."

Maj. Gen. Doyle E. Larson, then commander of the Electronic Security Command, spoke at the dedication, during which it was noted that Rodney "was killed in action when his EC-47 was shot down by enemy fire while flying a combat mission from Pleiku Air Base."

A brochure distributed in conjunction with the ceremony said he "was promoted posthumously to Technical Sergeant." It also alludes to the fact that during a brief assignment with the 6993rd Security Squadron at Kelly "he worked on several projects concerning the Vietnam conflict" and his "enthusiastic approach to these problems resulted in commendations for his unit by several national level agencies."

Rodney earned a Bronze Star and Air Medal, among other decorations, for his Vietnam service.

Sylvia remembers performing in Miami Beach clubs during World War II when bands played only from 9 p.m. to midnight. "They had to turn off all the lights in the city because of the fear of submarines," she says. "That was terrible."

Sylvia organized her own band, called "Sylvia's Trio," following the death of her second husband, who she says was the true love of her life.

"He was such a good guy," she says. "I've had some dancing dates since he died, but I could never find another one like him."

"Before we married, he had gorgeous show girls after him all the time. I don't know how I got him. He had a trunk full of pictures of beautiful women that I made him get rid of after the wedding."

Sylvia's trio performed at the Tiki Club on the Tamiami Trail for years and at other venues in Florida until she was well into her 80s.

"We played mostly the music of the '40s, waltzes, fox

trots, tangos, cha-chas, and rumbas," she says. "No one plays that here. I'm still waiting to see someone on Tybee do a rumba. But there are a lot of good dancers here. I'm trying to teach some of the men to do the rumba and a lot of them want to learn."

During recent years, she lived with her son, Gary, in Miami, but often visited her daughter Pat on Tybee and was finally convinced to move up just after her 90th birthday party in Miami on Feb. 5.

More than a hundred people showed up to honor her at the big birthday bash in the Miami Moose Club, where Sylvia is a life member. She's also a life member of the VFW and Miami Musicians Union.

"That was a great party," she says. "It was a catered affair with wonderful food and balloons and music and everything. Lots of people came. I'll never forget it."

Due to deteriorating night vision, Sylvia has swapped driving a car for another mode of transportation on her evening island outings.

It's a little electric scooter which she navigates to and from her residence, parking it on the sidewalk outside whatever lounge she is frequenting. "I'm crazy about that thing," she laughs. "Everyone waves and says hello to me when I pass. I don't even know half the people who speak to me but it's great."

Sylvia has become a popular dance partner for islanders. Most are astounded when they learn her true age, a number that still surprises her.

"I certainly don't feel like I'm 90, but I can't keep it a secret because people are always telling everyone how old I am," she laughs.

"A lot of people say if they can be like me at 90, they won't mind growing old. Even my grandson told me he never felt he wanted to be 90, but when he looked at me, he said 'Grandma, you do all right. If I can be like you at 90, I think I'll make it.'"

POSTSCRIPT: See the following description of Sylvia's 91st birthday party in Doc's Bar. Later reports concerning the death of her son, Rodney H. Gott, revealed that the wreckage of the plane on which he was killed was discovered in a mountainous area of Laos in the fall of 1969 and that it was shot down by enemy fire. His name is listed on Panel 33W, Line 65 of the Vietnam Veterans Memorial Wall in Washington, D.C.

Birthday cake awaits Miss Sylvia.

Celebrating Life at Island Bar

The party at her favorite island night spot continued until the wee morning hours as she danced the night away.

That's standard stuff for Sylvia Gott, a fixture at Doc's Bar on Tybee where you'll find her every weekend, seated at a table beside the bandstand near the entrance.

She always looks quite regal wearing fashionable silk dresses which set her apart from the typical clientele, most of whom don the standard Tybee attire of T-shirts and shorts or jeans, with sporadic summer appearances by tipsy bikini-clad bimbos.

Sylvia holds court for regulars who drop by to pay her homage, chat, or ask her to dance at this eclectic island watering hole.

When neither dancing nor conversing, she keeps meticulous time with a tambourine or maracas, accompanying house musician Charlie Sherrill who calls her his "percussion section." "She's just great," says Sherrill. "She helps me keep the rhythm when I get a little off."

Sylvia Gott celebrates birthday at Doc's.

But Feb. 5, was something special.

It was her birthday.

Sylvia was 91 years young on that day, and Doc's was the obvious place for her to celebrate.

Crowds converged on the bar early and stayed late, hovering around her table with an assortment of gifts, many of the liquid variety since Sylvia is known to quaff a bit of the bubbly (make that vodka and water if you want to curry her favor) during her evening festivities.

Most in attendance were less than half Sylvia's age, but few could muster even that percentage of her energy.

They lingered for her late-night cutting of the huge cake placed on the pool table in the center of the dance floor but were pretty much partied out by midnight when many began wobbling unsteadily towards the exit.

In her typically effervescent manner, Sylvia was still going strong until the early morning hours, dancing, chatting, and keeping time with the music. They don't make 'em like her anymore.

"I love the music, and I've always loved to dance," she says. "I love to listen to Charlie. He's such a great musician...too good for Tybee."

Sylvia's opinion should not be taken lightly. She has made her share of appearances as a professional musician for more than three quarters of a century.

She was proficient on the piano at the age of 6, then took up the trumpet which she played in her father's concert band at 12 and continued to perform with that band through her high school years in Stuart, Florida, a small town where she knew most of the people way back when.

"But everything there has changed now," she sighs. "At my age I've outlived 'em all."

Ultimately, she traded her trumpet for the drums. "They were a lot easier on my lips," says the laughing, long-time musician.

Sylvia performed in bands with her husband for 41 years until his death in 1966, then organized her own group, "Sylvia's Trio," entertaining throughout south Florida until she was well into her 80s.

She is justifiably proud of the fact that she was named a life member of the Miami Musicians Union as well as the Miami Moose Club and VFW.

Her only lament regarding island musicians is that they don't play the music in which she specialized... traditional, tangos, waltzes, fox trots, cha-chas, and rumbas.

Sylvia Gott at 91st birthday celebration.

"I'm still waiting to see someone on Tybee do a rumba," she says. "There are a lot of good dancers here, and I'm trying to teach some of the men to do the rumba."

But whatever dance they're doing you can bet that Sylvia will be there, gliding gracefully round the floor just as she did on her 91st birthday.

Miss Sylvia blows out candles on her birthday cake.

For Sylvia and a precious few like her, age is nothing but a number.

POSTSCRIPT: Miss Sylvia continued to frequent Doc's Bar, always ensconced at her own table beside the bandstand, offering her percussion accompaniment for years. Crowds gathered at the bar to honor her at birthday celebrations into her mid-90s. Miss Sylvia Gott passed away on Oct. 30, 2014. She was 101 years young.

Appendix

The articles in this volume were originally published in the Savannah Morning News. The original publication dates for each are as follows:

1. Nickie Alexander 9/9/2005
2. Dan DeLoach.. 4/1/1997
3. George McDonald 12/24/1997
4. John O'Neill.. 4/18/97
5. Sally Bostwick 5/12/1998
6. Albert Seidl.. 12/17/1998
7. Sinbad 10/1/1996
8. Linda Odom... 1/15/96
9. Michael Hosti 2/7/1997
10. George Oliver 11/9/1997
11. Marlyce Kling 8/26/99
12. Bob Martin 10/10/1996
13. Mike Ryan 9/30/1999
14. Jenny Orr 6/4/1999
15. Steven Scheer...................................... 6/19/1997
16. Leonard "Sandman" Miller 9/17/1998
17. The Chu Sisters.................................... 2/19/1998
18. Lance Smith 3/22/1997
19. Burke Day 3/16/1997
20. Sylvia Gott 8/5/1999

Acknowledgements

Like all writers, I am indebted to a number of people who contributed substantially to bringing this book to fruition.

I want to thank Suzi Fuchs, a former print journalist and dear friend now living in Arizona, for her suggestions and editing early on in this effort.

I am also grateful to newspaper columnist and author Ben Goggins for his astute editing, thoughtful advice, and kind words of encouragement.

Miranda Pagan was especially helpful in re-typing old columns which were not preserved in my computer files, while Tybee environmentalist, author, calligrapher, and artist Mallory Pearce created the caricatures of the subjects of each chapter.

Layout Designer Lauren Clackum, known hereabouts fondly as the "Princess of Pages," did all the nitty-gritty formatting and layout for the book in a timely and professional manner which made her extraordinary craftsmanship seem deceptively effortless.

I am also grateful to all those who encouraged me to continue with this project along the way.

Without each of you this book would likely never have seen the light of day.

www.ingramcontent.com/pod-product-compliance
Lightning Source LLC
Chambersburg PA
CBHW071941210726
48293CB00004BA/1457
* 9 7 8 1 9 5 9 5 6 3 0 3 7 *